Frank Reaugh

Painter to the Longhorns

Number Seven: The Joe and Betty Moore Texas Art Series

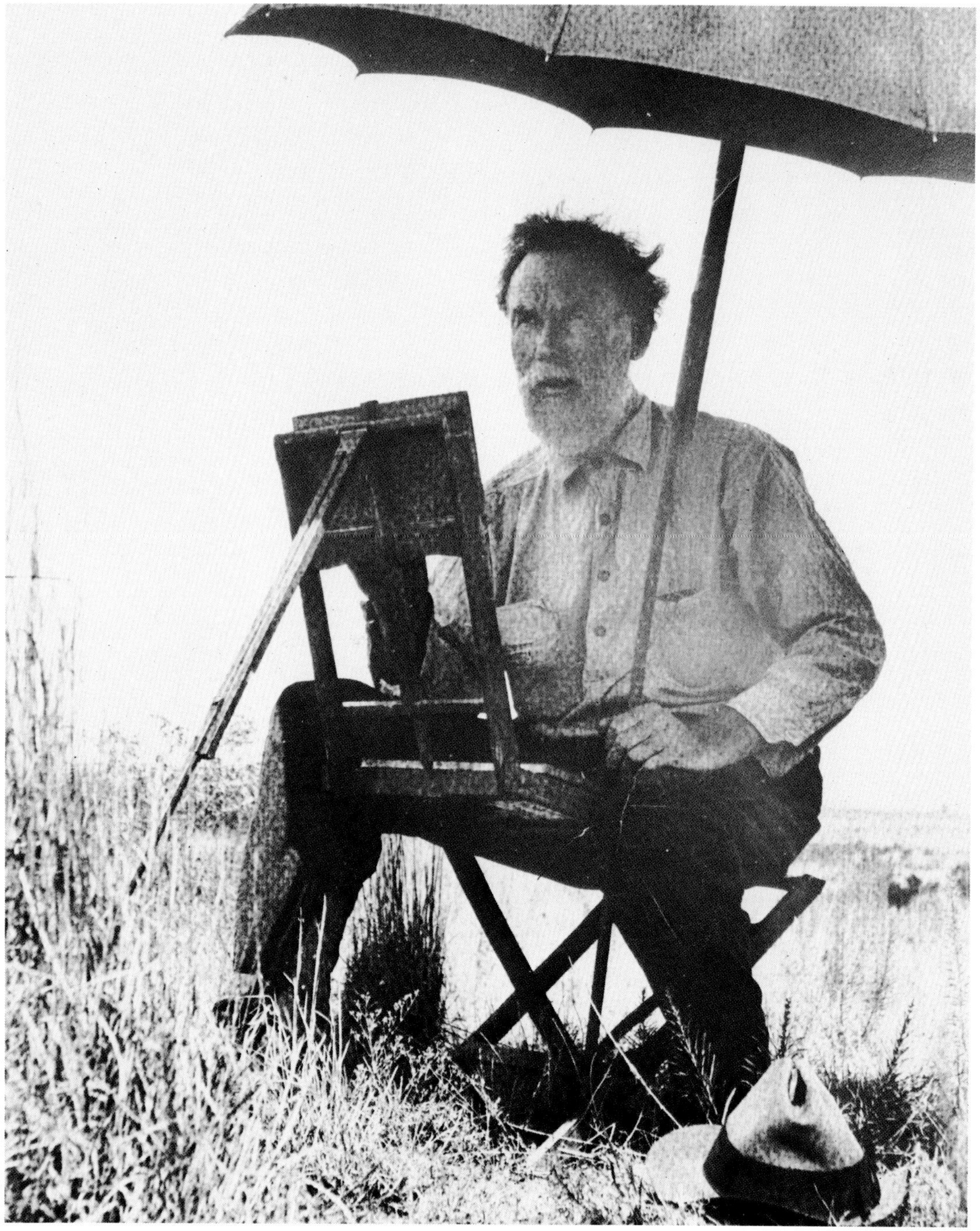

Frank Reaugh

Painter to the Longhorns

Introduction by Donald L. Weismann

Texas A&M University Press, *College Station*

Library of Congress Cataloging in Publication Data

Reaugh, Frank.
Frank Reaugh, painter to the longhorns.

1. Reaugh, Frank. 2. Longhorn cattle in art.
3. West (U.S.) in art. I. Weismann, Donald L.
II. Title.
NC139.R39A4 1985 741'092'4 85-40051
ISBN 0-89096-236-7

Manufactured in the United States of America
FIRST EDITION

To Frank H. Wardlaw

Contents

Introduction

A scant one hundred years after the adoption of the American Declaration of Independence, and only forty years after the Battle of San Jacinto and the founding of the Republic of Texas, a covered wagon bound out of Illinois carried a boy of fifteen into Texas. The boy was Franklin Reaugh, only child of George Washington and Clarinda Spilman Reaugh, who were seeking a new life in the Southwest. It was all new, mile after mile, to the young Franklin, but not to his father, who had gone overland to California eleven years before, seeking a fortune that eluded him. Young Franklin, who always had "a liking for drawing,"[1] as he put it, watched the passing country for subjects for his pencil as the wagon kept heading south and into the westerlies, across the Arkansas River above Fort Smith, out of Arkansas, then through Oklahoma Territory, and into the Lone Star State.

Sixty years after crossing the line, and long after he had shortened his name to the simpler Frank, Frank Reaugh (pronounced Ray), recalled that "in Texas there were motifs in plenty. There were no mountains in sight, but there was illimitable distance, and there were skies that were beautiful, grand or awe-inspring."[2] For us now, with the legacy of thousands of pastels and oil paintings that Reaugh has left us, the evidence is clear that his sympathy and admiration for the magnificence of those heralding skies and the call of those illimitable distances only intensified with his growing years.

[1]Frank Reaugh, *Biographical*, pamphlet (El Sibil [Dallas], 1936).
[2]Ibid.

The Reaugh family took hold on a small ranch in Kaufman County just southeast of Dallas. "Our fence," Frank said, "was the only one in sight . . . on that open range, wild and free."[3] It was during these early days of the very early 1880s that he began his studies of cattle. The subjects were all around him—a living part of the natural environment of rich, free grass pasture. And of all the grazing cattle it was the big, longhorned steers brought up from the stock ranches of south Texas that commanded his attention and deepened an abiding interest (plates 2, 18, 33, and 43). For most of his life an autodidact in matters of art, young Reaugh made use of whatever came to hand with promises of help toward the perfection he sought. "I had never yet seen an original painting, or any good work in color," he says of that time, "but I had studied carefully and avidly engravings and photo reproductions of good work . . . hence, my first pictorial visions were in black and white."[4]

Although it never suffices to know which other artists' works an artist admired—or even, at times, copied—in order to understand and appreciate his work, such knowledge can contribute to an understanding. In Reaugh's case he is entirely straightforward in telling us which artists, early in his career, he admired and learned from—even though the examples of their work that he saw came through the colorless translations available in photographs and engravings.

Among those he cites are the Americans Frederick Edwin

[3]Ibid.
[4]Ibid.

Church (1826–1900), who, although he painted scenes from our mountainous West, preferred exotic landscapes and excelled in panoramic visions of great expanse; Frederick Stuart Church (1842–1924), whose illustrations and drawings of animals were made available to Reaugh through reproductions in *Harper's Magazine*; George Fuller (1822–84), a successful New York and Boston portraitist and figure and landscape painter who eventually turned to farming; Abbot Thayer (1849–1921), best known for his paintings of animals, landscapes, and idealized women. Thayer's knowledge of animals was profound, and with his brother Gerald he wrote a treatise, *Protective Coloration of the Animal Kingdom*, that served as a valuable resource for perfecting military camouflaging during the First World War. Of the English painters important in his early studies, Reaugh mentions J. M. W. Turner (1775–1851), a master of poetic and visionary interpretations of land- and seascapes who personally supervised engravings made from his original works, and Sir Edwin Henry Landseer (1802–73), one of the most popular English painters of animals, remembered most for his sentimental pictures of dogs, which, if Reaugh saw any reproduced versions of them, would have been of no consequence to him. It is more likely that such subjects as Landseer's *The Stag at Bay* found resonance in him. Of the French painters it was Camille Corot (1796–1875) and Rosa Bonheur (1822–99) whose landscapes and animal paintings held interest for Reaugh. With Corot it was the early landscapes painted out-of-doors. With Bonheur, it was perhaps not so much the shallow romantic idealism of her painted animals as it was the dynamism of some of her compositions, of which her widely celebrated *Horse Fair* is an excellent example and one which Reaugh specifically mentions as having held a special attraction for him. It may even have directly influenced such works as his *Weather Prophets* (plate 57). He mentions only one Dutch painter, Paulus Potter (1625–54), whose work in engraved and etched versions he admired during his early career. Potter, who worked in The Hague and Amsterdam, has often been considered one of the finest Dutch painters of animals during the seventeenth century. His landscapes are rendered with an uncommonly sensitive awareness of the variations of light and atmosphere and their effects on the appearance of the everyday subjects he painted. We know that Reaugh saw and carefully studied one of the black-and-white versions of Potter's life-size painting, *Young Bull*, commissioned by the Prince of Nassau. He could also have seen versions of Potter's *Meadow with Oxen* and *Landscape with Cattle*.

It has not been unusual for artists to make use of engravings, mezzotints, and other reproductions of other artists' work as part of their means to perfection of their own art. One of the greatest of American painters, John Singleton Copley (1738–1815), living in colonial Boston and at the time far from access to original works of the masters, worked first from prints and engravings. And the perenially fascinating mystic poet and artist William Blake (1757–1827) of London based most of his figure composition on the sculpture and painting of Michaelangelo, whose works Blake knew only by way of engravings after the originals.

With the invention of the camera and permanent photographic prints, the camera in the hands of painters has proved a powerful means for extending their grasp of the visual world. Reaugh himself was a skilled photographer, as witnessed to by hundreds of his four-by-five-inch glass negatives preserved in the Panhandle-Plains Historical Museum in Canyon, Texas. Used as an art medium in itself as well as a "sketch" and research medium for subsequent paintings, the photograph has served painters for the last one hundred and fifty years. The long list of artists who were photographers as well as painters—as Reaugh was—includes artists of such varied persuasions as Edvard Munch (1863–1944), the Norwegian expressionist; Thomas Eakins (1844–1916), the American realist; Edgar Degas (1834–1917), the French precursor of impressionism; Albert Bierstadt (1830–1902), the German-American romantic realist painter of the American West; and hundreds more right up to the present.

No matter the kind or quality of photographic or engraved works that found their ways to the young Reaugh, he took from them only what helped him see better what was right there in front of him: the open range lighted and shaded like a great stage, peopled by the few cowboys working among the moving grazing cattle (plates 25 and 53). For Reaugh, unlike his contemporaries Frederic Remington and Charles Russell, it was the animals more than the cowboys that summoned him out onto the prairie with his pencils, paints, and pastels. He had measured and drawn his first live models, Tom and Jerry, the work oxen he drove on the little ranch near Terrell, and he had managed to come by a two-bit book about animal anatomy—published in England, he thought, by a man named Rowney, or something like that.

Frank Reaugh, on his own and without knowledge of or desire to mimic the French impressionists who painted out-of-doors directly from nature, simply became his own style of *plein air* painter (plates 7, 15, 31, and 48). We are apt to forget that painting directly from nature, except in the cases of portraiture and still life, was not common until the nineteenth century. It is true that artists from way back *sketched* directly from their out-of-doors subjects. But their finished paintings were most often accomplished in the studio, the sketches providing data and guides rather than the living spirit and ambient light of nature as directly perceived. John Constable (1776–1837), the innovative English landscape painter of such masterpieces as *The Hay Wain* and *Hampstead Heath*, may have been one of the very first to commit himself to painting landscapes while seated in the landscape itself. And it may be of some significance to note that because he did this, and because his paintings celebrated such common incidents of rural life as sunlight on the back of a horse or the look of damp moss on a rotting stump, his paintings avoided the studied flamboyance or academic idealism of his contemporaries' studio works. No wonder that Constable's humble and intimate observations—comparable in spirit to those of Frank Reaugh—went so long unregarded, just as Reaugh's have.

The French impressionists (Sisley, Pissarro, Monet, and others), at least for generous parts of their careers, painted almost exclusively out-of-doors. Their first exhibition of this new *plein air* painting was held—and ridiculed—in a vacant photographer's studio in Paris only about seven or eight years before young Reaugh was outside, oblivious to all that, and painting alone on the prairie around Terrell in Texas.

It was not long after these first seminars with the animals on the range that Reaugh discovered his "fondness for painting Texas cattle in their natural wildness; subjects free from any influence or suggestion of man; resulting in such pictures as *The Monarch of the Plains*, *Dawn*, and *The Challenge*" (plate 30), as Reaugh reports in his short autobiography, published in 1936. "In the early eighties," he said, "I became acquainted with the brothers Frank and Romie Houston. Frank Houston was one of the great cattle kings of that day, handling hundreds of thousands of beef cattle per year; his herds were scattered well over West Texas and the Indian Territory. With all his big business interests he had an eye for the beauty and romance of the range. Through his interest and courtesy I saw some of the greatest of the round-ups, and rode with the cattle on the trail; fitting me for such works as *The One O Round-up*, and the series *Twenty-Four Hours with the Herd*"[5] (plates 35–41).

Frank Reaugh came early to the principal subject matter

[5]Ibid

for his paintings—the Texas Longhorn—studying and sketching him singly, in groups, and in the herd and, as he has said, "in the beauty of the great Southwest as God has made it." He got to know the Longhorns at first hand, their nature and habits, their characteristic spots and markings, and their rich and varied color. It may be true that the authentic and poetic visions of the Longhorn at roundup time, which Reaugh created for us in oils and pastels in the early 1880s, are the only authentic studies made of such subjects at that time—made on the same ground where they grazed, slept, and stampeded.

In 1884 Frank Reaugh, already an accomplished artist at the age of twenty-four, scraped together his little savings, including those he had put aside as a short-term schoolteacher, got some local backing, and went off as a student to the School of Fine Arts in Saint Louis, Missouri. Now, this sort of meeting of the largely self-taught, accomplished artist with the institutionalized programs of name-brand art schools has long been a phenomenon of interest to this writer. It is of no less interest in the case of Frank Reaugh.

This writer, for years director of university art departments in Kentucky and Texas, is familiar with the particular brand of whimsical insecurity felt by genuine artists who attend as students or teach in academic situations. He has found this most prevalent in the cases of accomplished painters and sculptors who have come to their acclaim, often national, with little benefit of formal schooling beyond high school—certainly without study in known and respected schools of art. It would seem that an admirable innocence of what actually goes on in a lot of university art departments and schools of art fosters in these "deprived" artists a mysterious and unfounded respect mixed with a fear of being "found out," so to speak. And this same whimsical insecurity often evidences itself even in situations outside academia where the artist finds himself merely hobnobbing with university- and professional school–bred people: lawyers, "graphics design specialists," businessmen, doctors—women out of Bryn Mawr, Smith, and Vassar; men out of Harvard, Princeton, Yale, and our own University of Texas. In some cases these artists manage to continue with their art by assuming quiet or loud protective attitudes of superiority in relation to the people around. In other cases they save up their money and go off to some university or professional school, often to learn things quite outside their art. In still other cases, already accomplished artists remain so involved with further developing their art that that other world, recognized or not, commands almost none of their attention and only what is unavoidably required of their time.

So, in 1884 Frank Reaugh went off to the Saint Louis School of Art for a few months and then returned to Terrell. There are those who speculate that this short affiliation with a professional school was aimed at impressing some of the cultivated people of Terrell—enough that they would take art lessons from him. This writer chooses to guess that the idea of going to school was half his and half that of others—some interested folks of Terrell and, almost certainly, Reaugh's mother, who throughout his life believed in and worked for his development as an artist.

However that may have been, upon his return to Terrell, Reaugh resumed his outdoor sketching and painting, ranging farther and farther beyond the limits of Kaufman County. A group of women of the town, some of whom had perhaps backed his schooling in Saint Louis, got together with Reaugh and formed the Frank Reaugh Art Study Club. It appears that his first regular teaching was done under the auspices of this club. A little later, in a printed statement addressed "To My Patrons," he set forth some of his convictions regarding art and his aims in teaching. "I do not teach art with a view of making artists except in the rarest cases," the statement reads, "and I do not teach it as a mere accomplishment ever. Art should be taught with the view of training both the vision and the mind, and especially the mind. It should be made as important a part of learning as mathematics. No faculty is more used or more capable of development than the sense of sight. . . . No intellectual attainment is more valuable than the power of judging the fitness of things as to form, color and proportion. . . . Mere manual dexterity follows as a [*sic*] incident. Art is creative. Its study develops powers of thought and reasoning, rather than any trick of hand. In working from nature, as the serious artist must do, the hand is rarely called on to do the same thing twice; it must obey the will. Study art, not to do, but to know, then it may be that what you do will be worth while."[6] With all the romantic qualities evident in Reaugh's paintings, the same creative union of vision and thought set forth in this statement may provide the best key to their power to move us as well as inform us in distinctive ways.

Slowly but steadily Reaugh was now selling some paintings. The prices of his medium-size pastels ranged from twenty to forty or fifty dollars—ridiculously low in light of today's outrageously inflated prices for works that are often greatly inferior to his. Reaugh was also realizing some income from his teaching. A frugal, single man of simple wants, he had enough money by November of 1888 to sail from New York to Antwerp, on his one and only trip abroad.

Unlike another American painter, Albert P. Ryder (1847–1917), who made his sole trip to Europe just a few years before Reaugh and who is said to have been impressed only by the moonlight on the sea, Reaugh was impressed by the works of a variety of European masters. For a short time he studied at the Julien School of Art in Paris and became aware—to what extent we cannot be certain—of the revolutionary work of the French impressionists. What appears most to have engaged his interests were the works of eighteenth- and nineteenth-century artists whose works he saw in the Louvre. Of these, he was most taken with those of Maurice Quentin de La Tour (1704—88), the celebrated portraitist who worked almost exclusively in pastel, and by those of Anton Mauve (1838–88), the Dutch landscape and animal painter. He must also have been deeply impressed by Turner's atmospheric landscapes, which up to that time he had seen only in engravings after the originals.

Technically, Reaugh was most concerned with La Tour's use of the pastel medium, the medium Reaugh had already adopted as his principal means of expression. It was, however, the light-saturated bucolic landscapes of Mauve that resonated most vibrantly with Reaugh's aesthetic preoccupations. To learn more about the elusive qualities of color that, to Reaugh, made Mauve's paintings the subtle orchestrations they were, he traveled to The Hague, where he could see, close up, a great variety of his work. "Of all the work I saw abroad," Reaugh said, "I was most impressed by that of Anton Mauve."[7]

It perhaps does not matter to us living during these last years of the twentieth century that the name of Anton Mauve now rarely turns up in histories of art. And it perhaps does not matter, either, that when his name does come up it is rapidly dismissed as that of a relatively negligible and sentimental painter. But we know that any artist worth his salt learns from whatever sources he or she can—taking what helps and leaving the rest. So Frank Reaugh, almost a hundred years ago, found help and inspiration waiting for him in the work of this now almost forgotten Dutch painter. And lest we overlook how unpredictably the wide-flung net of destiny brings together people, artists of disparate natures and intent, we

[6]Flyer announcing Reaugh's "Lessons in Art, in the Studio and Out," Oak Cliff, Texas, n.d.

[7]Reaugh, *Biographical*.

should remember that just six years before Frank Reaugh studied the Mauve paintings in The Hague, Vincent van Gogh had studied with his cousin—the same Anton Mauve, in the same town. Van Gogh went on from there to create some of the most turbulent images of the French landscape, intense reflections of his own anxiety. Reaugh went on to paint some of the most subtle and beguiling images of the great Southwest lands while the Longhorn still roamed free—reflections of his own inner peace and admiration for what he was sure God had bequeathed to all of us (plates 12, 32, 44, and 51).

While in Europe Reaugh also visited Spain, but of that part of his sojourn little has been reported. Perhaps it was covered by his general statement concerning his overseas adventure: "Contact with the world was the most valuable thing I gained."[8] One must wonder, however, how the masterpieces of Velásquez, Brueghel, El Greco, and Goya hanging there in Madrid's Prado affected him and if, as he went along Spain's valleys, he thought of the Longhorns back home in Texas and their distant Spanish derivation.

Of the significant Paris Exposition of 1889, Reaugh wrote only that he saw the World's Fair there—nothing specific about the extensive exhibition or about Alexandre Eiffel's tower erected in the Champs-de-Mars for the Exposition.

Frank Reaugh returned to Texas in the summer of 1889 and almost immediately set out on another of his sketching and painting trips into the range country of West Texas. As time went on these trips were extended over most of the *Llano Estacado*, the southerly part of the Great Plains plateau of West Texas and eastern New Mexico, called in English the Staked Plains. These trips, Reaugh said, became pretty nearly annual after his return from Europe. "I never had a desire to work or live in the North or East," he said, "though for the first 20 years after my return from France I exhibited annually in the Chicago Art Institute, the Pennsylvania and National Academies and other galleries in the East."[9] And in those years his work was honored in such national exhibitions as the Annual American Artists' shows in Chicago, where it was hung in the center of the line in the main gallery. It was shown at the Chicago and the Saint Louis world's fairs in 1893 and 1903, all entries having been judged by competent national juries. Two of the only forty-four works sold at the Chicago World's Fair were Reaugh pastels.

In 1890 the Reaugh family moved into the Dallas area, to a generous two-story house at 110 East Eighth Street in the Oak Cliff section. Back of the house Reaugh and his father built a separate place, a studio-workshop and living quarters for the bachelor artist. A frame structure sheathed with galvanized iron, it was soon dubbed "Old Ironsides." Rising above the one-story structure was an ample tower or lookout, open on all sides, Frank Reaugh's sleeping quarters—in the open air as he preferred.

Once he was in the environs of burgeoning Dallas and within easy reach of friends and the inquisitive, interest in the man and his art rapidly increased. In time he enthusiastically responded to repeated requests to teach his art to others. With a group of girls aged nine to fifteen and their parents, he founded a club, the Stringinian Club, really a sort of continuing seminar in art and nature. Should anyone wonder why all the members of the seminars were girls, this writer, a recognized artist a decade before Reaugh died in 1945, reminds himself of how things were back then: If boys, like this writer, showed an interest in the arts that superseded interest in baseball, football, and hot-rods, then that boy was thought to be an

[8]Alice Bab Stroud and Modena Stroud Dailey, *F. Reaugh—Texas Longhorn Painter*, 1962, p. 28.

[9]Reaugh, *Biographical.*

oddball, effeminate, a sissy. It was the girls back then who were supposed to be interested in art; the boys should be getting in shape for the rough-and-ready world. Of course, things have changed since then—with little loss to the male's macho image of himself.

Frank Reaugh spent a generous part of his career as a teacher, first on an informal basis, then with a well-conceived plan. As director of the Dallas School of Fine Arts, he taught organized classes in "landscape and animal sketching" in his Oak Hill studio. In an early printed circular advertising the school—complete with back sheet ads for "Artist Material, Picture Frames and Wall Paper by the J. E. Grant Company," and for "A Complete New Stock of Fine Footwear" offered by the Flippen Shoe Company—Reaugh, working with a board of "counselors," set forth the objectives of the school. They read very simply: ". . . to give to students the best advantages for the thorough study of art at a reasonable rate of tuition, or if necessary, to students deemed worthy of it, to give tuition free. Also, it aims through exhibitions, lectures, and every other means in its power to foster the interest in art in the community at large." And Reaugh, one of the most quietly powerful early forces in building an art consciousness in Dallas and beyond, solicited public support. Under the heading "Patrons" in the same circular, the invitation is extended: "Believing there were many of our citizens, who, though unable to send students to the school, would nevertheless like to encourage the growth of good art in our community, the counselors have invited such to become patrons of the school by contributing an annual sum of $5.00, with the understanding that they shall be entitled to full privileges of all lectures, exhibitions or other entertainments of general interest that the school may give."[10]

Along with teaching regularly in the Dallas School of Fine Arts, Reaugh organized and conducted field trips spent in studying and sketching directly from nature. These trips were usually scheduled to last a month or more, and certain regulations were rigorously enforced. For instance, each student was allowed no more than thirty pounds of luggage, including drawing and painting equipment. No cots or tents were allowed. Reaugh expected his students, young and old, male and female, to roll out their blankets at the end of the day and sleep roofless under the stars, emulating the ways of the cowboy on the move. And he was a richly experienced guide and teacher in matters of living out while working and moving across the range. As Alice Bab Stroud and Modena Stroud Dailey report in their book *F. Reaugh—Texas Longhorn Painter*,

> Mr. Reaugh once [in the early thirties] reminisced about these annual trips to John Williams Rogers, as follows: "I have been making these trips to West Texas for exactly fifty years. . . . In '83, I went with a mule team and covered wagon. After that, through the 80's, I went with cattlemen, stopping in cowboy camps and generally using a buckboard to get around in. Among the pictures of mine which grew out of material gained on the early trips are 'Driving the Herd' [plate 35] and 'The Round-up.'
>
> "For several seasons after my return from Europe in 1890, I made trips in a Studebaker hack, buying a couple of horses at the Monday stray sales, and selling them again after my return. One of these trips was to the Llano River . . . another West to the plains. During the season of 1909–10, a collection of sixty sketches from one of these trips was sent on a north circuit and shown in St. Louis, Detroit, Grand Rapids, Chicago and Indianapolis."[11]

Between 1916 and 1920 Reaugh with students and friends made a number of trips by rail to Colorado, Wyoming, and Arizona. "The Rockies are fine," Reaugh said, "but I like Texas

[10] *Dallas School of Fine Arts, Circular for Years 1899–1900.*

[11] Stroud and Dailey, *F. Reaugh*, pp. 47, 48.

better. Forms are more interesting and color as varied and more harmonious."[12] In the years after 1920 up to only a short time before his death in 1945, Frank Reaugh and student friends made trips to the Grand Canyon via El Paso, Tucson, and Phoenix, returning through Socorro, Albuquerque, and Amarillo; up the Rio Grande and back through the Organ and Sacramento mountains; into the Davis Mountains and through the Big Bend country; to Acoma, Taos, and the Conejas Canyon, Colorado; to Double Mount, Fort McKavett, the Canadian, Tule Canyon, Blanco Canyon; and around and back, always, to his studio in Oak Hill. Once the Studebaker hack, mules, and horses were put to rest, Reaugh and his loyal fellow artist-travelers made their way in Ford automobiles, touring models, of course, with given names such as "The Cicada," "Cricket," and "Jumping Spider." And always Reaugh returned with dozens of sketches, many of which proved to be finished pastel paintings of a vanishing way of life.

An account of Frank Reaugh's life limited to his work as a pioneer Texas artist would, by itself, make a rich and significant story. But there was much more to this extraordinary man. In a rustic homespun way he shared some of the characteristics of such historically great artists as Leone Battista Alberti and Leonardo da Vinci of fifteenth-century Italy. Besides being a painter, Reaugh was an amateur naturalist, a photographer, a philosopher, and an inventor. And lest this association of Reaugh with such great names as Alberti and Leonardo be deemed unwarranted or even preposterous, we can, rather, associate him with a significant number of celebrated American artists whose lives and works attest to the same many-sided character as Reaugh's. For instance, there is Robert Fulton (1765–1815), a painter who was also a gunsmith and canal engineer and who worked at making underwater torpedoes, submarines, and a variety of machinery—even though we remember best his building of the steamboat *Clermont*, the first commercially successful one used in American waters. We can think of Samuel F. B. Morse (1791—1872), a portrait and history painter who developed his own version of the electric telegraph, devised the Morse Code, invented a special kind of water pump, experimented with submarine cable telegraphy, and, with the help of John Draper, introduced the daguerrotype into the United States. There is Charles Willson Peale (1741–1827), portrait painter, naturalist, watchmaker, silversmith, and inventor of new methods used in taxidermy, new types of eyeglasses and false teeth, a velocipede, and the polygraph. There are John Rogers (1829–1904), sculptor, machinist, and engineer; Thomas Eakins (1844–1916), painter and sculptor, who, with Eadweard Muybridge, invented an early forerunner of the stroboscopic camera used to study humans and animals in action. And that would be to say nothing of present-day "hi-tech" visuals artists, whose work often presupposes exercises in higher mathematics, physics, psychology, microelectronics, and linguistics.

With Frank Reaugh, born the year Abraham Lincoln became president, the many-sidedness of his make-up appears to have exerted itself as a natural consequence of his personal concern for nature and art. In February, 1920, he filed with the United States Patent Office for a patent of his "Lap Easel." It was granted in December, 1923. Because the descriptive language of the patent document and the described lap easel itself so well reflect the practical element in Reaugh's make-up, this writer is inclined to quote from it. In part it reads:

> Be it known that I, FRANK REAUGH . . . have invented certain new and useful Improvements in Lap Easels, of which the following is a specification.
>
> This invention is an improved lap easel adapted to be supported primarily in or over the lap of a person in sitting posture,

[12] Ibid., p. 49.

the top or upper part of the easel being supported or braced from the ground.

My improved construction in its preferred form is adapted for outdoor or indoor use in sketching, drawing or painting and is light, compact and strong. The three leg support insures the requisite steadiness and the back leg is not only adjustable to permit the supporting of the drawing board at the desired angle, but is foldable to facilitate convenient carrying or storage and is so designed and fastened that it will stay in adjusted position. The easel may be held firmly in position by knee pressure leaving both hands free and the knee pressure in holding the easel may also hold the handle or staff of an umbrella or sunshade. The joints of the back leg are under spring tension which may be adjusted and the back leg, when in folded position, permits of the convenient supporting of the easel on a table or in any other position with the lower ends of the legs in approximately the same horizontal plane. The entire construction is easily and cheaply built and cannot very easily get out of order.

The Panhandle-Plains Historical Museum has among its collections one of Reaugh's patented lap easels, and this writer can attest to its ingenuity of design and serviceability. The fact that it is held in working position by a slight pressure of the knees contributes to a feeling of its being part of the artist as he or she works—much as a brush or a stick of pastel feels like an extension of the hand. And it is, of course, the kind of easel Reaugh would invent: one that would be surprisingly stable even in the gusts of rangeland winds. The photograph of Reaugh included in this volume (frontispiece) shows him using the easel, with umbrella and all, as he sketches in pastels out on the range. And since the umbrella has been mentioned, it may not be too much of a diversion at this point to have Reaugh himself tell of an incident involving it. In his pamphlet, *Paintings of the Southwest*, he says:

It was a warm day on the prairie, and after my walk as I sat at my easel under the shade of my big sketch umbrella the light breeze from the south was delightfully cool. I was prepared to sketch cattle, and as I expected, a little herd of about a dozen or so that were grazing a half or three-quarters of a mile to the north had seen us and were coming on the run to see what strange thing had invaded their grazing ground. At some 200 feet away they suddenly stopped, to stand and gaze from that safe distance; but, soon, with curiosity unsatisfied, with eyes and ears intent to catch the slightest move or sound, with nose thrust forward to test the strange odor on the air, cautiously, slowly, a few steps, and then a pause, and then a few steps more, they began to come closer and closer as I worked. All the little group were fine big cattle. The leader especially, was fine in form and carriage, and beautiful in color. I was working, working with my utmost speed to get him, when a sudden, unexpected gust of wind pulled my umbrella loose to go up a dozen feet in the air and then light on its edge and go rolling straight toward those cattle. They all stampeded at once, all but the leader. He was made of sterner stuff.

He braced himself and lowered his head to meet the thing. Few things would have rushed in on him; but the umbrella never hesitated. It came right on with a crazy, wobbling, bouncing gait that was disconcerting. He had never seen anything like it before, and he had no way of estimating its power or possibilities.

He was a powerful and a brave steer, prepared to fight, but this time, at the last minute he lost his nerve. With a bawl of terror that was almost a shriek, he whirled and rushed away with the rest of the herd.[13]

Now, although it may not be possible to determine the inventor or inventors of pastel, that chalk-like medium with ranges of color and value equal to those of oil paint, Frank Reaugh, working with others, perfected what he called "The Reaugh Pastel." He describes this in a little publication, *Pastel*:

[13]Frank Reaugh, *Paintings of the Southwest by Frank Reaugh—Notes by the Painter* (Dallas: Wilkinson Printing Company, n.d.), pp. 15, 16.

"The basic pigments are the best obtainable; the same as are used in artists' oil paints. To be sure of permanency, each lot of color is tested for . . . hardness and consistency before moulding, some colors requiring more gum, or different treatment from others. . . . It is our constant endeavor to mix and dry them in a way to secure the utmost strength and toughness. They are moulded by pressure, not by pouring. Even so, some pigments are by nature non-adhesive or brittle. Fortunately the most necessary colors can be made of the most suitable pigments." And then the final Reaugh practicality based in experience: "Our pastels are made in hexagon form so that they will not roll about as do round ones. Also because this form fits the fingers better."[14]

Early in the century Frank Reaugh invented and secured patents on the principles of a new kind of pump, the Limacon. In his descriptive pamphlet aimed at promoting the Limacon, he wrote that "the LIMACON principles, as applied to mechanics is [*sic*] the result of nearly ten years of study and experiment by the inventor, assisted by engineers of eminence and ability" and that the principles are "protected by broad basic patents in the United States, Canada and the principal countries of Europe."[15] How Reaugh became interested in inventing, developing, and promoting his Limacon pump is a matter for conjecture. It should not be surprising, however, that a person of Reaugh's ingenuity, with his closeness to and abiding interest in the forces of nature, should become interested in the mechanics of nature exemplified in the principles of a pump. Since Reaugh was known to be a wide and avid, though unsystematic, reader, it can be assumed that he knew of Blaise Pascal's seventeenth-century law that states that pressure applied to a confined fluid at any point is transmitted undiminished through the fluid in all directions and acts upon every part of the confining vessel at right angles to its interior surfaces and equally upon equal areas. But no matter how Reaugh came to invent a pump and assume an official role as secretary of the Limacon Pump and Motor Company of Dallas, it all attests to the creative many-sidedness of the man. And, incidentally, Limacon pumps were manufactured and their principles put on the market for companies interested in making use of them in compressors, blowers, meters, water and air motors, and other machines designed to move or utilize the motion of liquids and gasses.

It appears that Frank Reaugh was of a type—really a phenomenon—now called a "natural," or an "original." It is almost as if he was born to do what he did and that he did it—quite naturally. What he might have done had his mother and father not brought him to Texas with the last of the open range waiting to welcome him, perhaps only God could know. Maybe Frank Reaugh carried his ways with him, just as this writer believes Walter Prescott Webb, Texas' most celebrated historian, carried his with him. From the hard-scratch ground of his father's small Texas holding, Webb made a pilgrimage to the University of Chicago, but his ways brought him back to the University of Texas in Austin to write his first masterpiece, *The Great Plains* (1931), which set the whole American Historical Association on its deaf ear but eventually caused historians to hear and applaud him. Because a similarity appears to exist between some of the modes of operation of Walter Webb and Frank Reaugh, it may be in place to recall Webb's response to a question this writer asked him some years ago: "What do you do, Walter, when you get stuck and simply cannot proceed with your theorizing and interpretation of history?"

Almost without hesitation Webb answered, "I do a lot of things."

[14]Frank Reaugh, *Pastel*, pamphlet (Dallas: Reaugh Studios, 1927).

[15]*The Limacon*, pamphlet (Dallas: Limacon Pump and Motor Co., n.d.), p.1.

"Like what?" he was asked.

"Well, for example," Webb said, "I might take a big U.S. map, fold it in half, then half again and half again, and so on until I have a square, say about two or three inches across. Then let's say that on that square I see Great Falls, Montana; I take a stout pin and run it through that city—all the way through the layers of the folded map, pull out the pin, unfold the map and see what other places on the map got pierced. They'd be places like Youngstown, Ohio; Crookstown, Minnesota; Brownwood, Texas; Elko, Nevada; and Mission Valley, Iowa—and then I just look at that pattern of pinholes and think about what such a relation of places might suggest, or what I might read into the mechanically arrived-at pattern—just to get me going again."

It appears that Reaugh's various creative, inventive undertakings owed something to this ability to arrive at new perceptions by such seemingly incongruous procedures as Walter Webb recounted. Still and all, learning from such procedures often resulted in highly practical insights and solutions to problems. For Walter Webb, at one stage of his career, they may have contributed to his theory of the conquest of the great plains based on the crucial roles played by the inventions of barbed wire, the windmill, and the Colt six-shooter. For Frank Reaugh such procedures may have assisted his thinking about the possibility of the Limacon pump and the lap easel, a further perfection of the pastel medium, and his thinking about the relations existing between mathematics and art. Again, like Webb, Reaugh was a practical man. When he built the vault in which to store his paintings (called by its Spanish name, *El Sibil*), Reaugh was concerned that there be a way to check on the level of humidity in that protective space. Having learned from direct experience how the leather of boots, straps, and saddles respond to dampness and dryness, and himself being physically sensitive to this, he hung a leather strap in *El Sibil* and checked the humidity by simply feeling the strap—his own hygrometer.

With all Frank Reaugh's varied undertakings—he even played the guitar and piano—he was first and foremost a painter in pastels and oils. For more than sixty years this tall, handsome, soft-spoken Texan-by-adoption worked to create accurate and poetic images of the western country, with its dwindling herds of Longhorn cattle and the life that was then part of it all. Of a body of work that may number more than five thousand color sketches and paintings, most of them undated and ranging in size from two-by-three inches to over five feet across, it may be Reaugh's series called *Twenty-Four Hours with the Herd* that embodies his most serious concerns and gives evidence of his most sustained artistic efforts. This series of seven large pastel paintings, all painted after he was seventy years old and all in the collection of the Humanities Research Center at the University of Texas at Austin, are based upon the firsthand experience gained by Reaugh on his early trips to the western plains in the early eighties, when it was still a free-grass country. "There were a few scattered ranch houses, or range headquarters," Reaugh said, "with perhaps a corral or two nearby, but the range was open. The water holes were free for all, and the several trails that wound northward, the Chisholm trail and others less famous, swung this way or that to reach water, or a good crossing, but were not cut or diverted by lines of wire fence. The barbed wire had not come yet: nor the nestor: nor the sheep."[16]

That this series of paintings was of special significance to Reaugh himself is evidenced by his organizing special showings—really programs—built around the paintings. In a 1933 letter to Mrs. John L. Obrien of Waco he says: "I am getting

[16]Frank Reaugh and Clyde Walton Hill, *Prose Sketches*, pamphlet (Dallas, 1934).

ready to give another showing of my series 'Twenty-four Hours with the Herd.' Special lighting, descriptive reading, music. Will be glad if you can come, and bring friends. Admission $1.00." One would like to give Reaugh exclusive credit for inventing this early version of the multi-media program as another example of his "American ingenuity." However, we know there were forerunners—with programs perhaps not so all-embracing as Reaugh's, but forerunners just the same. Jacques Louis David (1748–1825), the French portrait and historical painter, had programmed his large neoclassical paintings, charged admission, and had viewers weep and wail before them. Benjamin West (1738–1820), the American ex-patriot painter of portraits and historical scenes, did very much the same in London. And there were others, notably the American cyclorama painters of the nineteenth century.

There are seven pastel paintings in the series *Twenty-four Hours with the Herd.* In sequence, their titles are: *Driving the Herd, Watering the Herd, Bedding the Herd, Guarding the Herd, The Stampede in the Canyon, Milling Cattle,* and *The Herd Moves On.* We are fortunate to have a publication, copyrighted in 1934 by Frank Reaugh, entitled *Twenty-four Hours with the Herd,* which includes what are called "Prose Sketches" accompanying the black-and-white reproductions of each of the paintings. The title page states that the text of these "Sketches" is "based partly on an earlier sketch by 'Hondo' and written jointly by the painter and by Clyde Walton Hill."

Since it is safe to assume that the result of this literary collaboration accurately reflects only what Reaugh himself deemed appropriate to say about his work, it should be of real significance to quote from it. From these prose counterparts to the paintings, which were read as part of Reaugh's multimedia programs, we can gain another insight into the descriptive nature of his artistic concerns. He does not talk about theories of composition, the psychology of visual perception, or the abstract function of color, line, or shape. The "metaphysics" of art are for someone other than Frank Reaugh to talk about.

Of *Driving the Herd* (plate 35), the first in the series of *Twenty-four Hours with the Herd,* Reaugh said:

The rocky hilltops are capped with shin-oaks; down on the creek a few cottonwood and hackberries grow. Occasionally there is a feathery mesquite, but for the most part the miles and miles of rolling prairie are covered only with a sparse growth of brownish gray bunch grass and golden yellow curly mesquite. On level stretches is a hint of mirage and on the far horizon a butte is pale and blue against the sky. All of it shimmers and glows opalescent under the intense light of the midday sun.

Along the side of a wide valley, coulee, almost a canyon, dug deep from the prairie's surface by uncounted centuries of rare but torrential rains, winds the dusty, much worn trail. Along it for half a mile before us extends a motley mass of varied color, red and yellow, black, brown and white, like an inland, slowly moving flood with surface of bobbing horns and swaying shoulders and lashing tails. Among them everywhere rise tributary streams of hazy dust, merging about to form the great dust cloud that rolls northwestward. Along the edges of the herd ride at intervals the browned and sinewy cowboys, gay of shirt beneath their open vests and red and blue bandanas and dusty broad-brimmed hats. . . . Far away at the head of the herd rides the boss, scanning with practiced eye the range ahead. At the rear with the remuda of extra mounts ride half a dozen men, keeping well apart, watching the wall of animals before them, calling sharply, now and then . . . to urge on the laggards and weaker steers, and stragglers that would stop to graze.

The air is heavy with the smell of dust and cattle. The silence of the mighty prairie is broken only by the dust-muffled tread of ten thousand hoofs making an all-pervading whisper as of wind among leaves; long horns rattle as they swing together, there is a creak of saddle leather while above and over all are the sharp and urgent calls of the cowboys, driving the herd.[17]

[17]Ibid.

Reaugh's references to the details of the pictured subject matter are all accurate and germane. The description he gives could be that of an actual situation—as if he were reporting from a low-flying helicopter as it approaches a live herd from the rear. He says nothing about his aesthetic judgements in selecting the subject matter he has chosen to show us and nothing about how he has organized it. And yet we see that he has made choices as to what he would and would not show, that he has summarized and composed the elements important to him. His artistic strategy of creating a great curving sweep from lower right, along the edge of the herd to a point against the sky at almost the center of the horizon and of the painting as a whole, thereby creating both a powerful feeling of movement and an illusion of deep space—all this must not have been deemed important enough for Reaugh to comment upon. Why make much of what he did naturally! Still, the employment of this sort of aesthetic strategy is a significant factor in Reaugh's work—a means by which these paintings are made more than colored photographs taken directly from life.

The second painting in the series is titled *Watering the Herd* (plate 36). This is what Frank Reaugh thought suitable to say about it:

> What a fountain of bliss is a watering place on the trail. Its waters ripple and sparkle in the sunlight with every passing breeze. Its little sandy beaches are bathing places for the birds, and in its shallows, the sedges and water weeds, though torn and trampled by many hoofs, are yet the playground for a myriad of bright winged, darting dragon flies. The water may be muddy, stained with the red of all the west and hot with all the day's heat from the summer sun, but if only it is sweet and free from gyp, it is well, and like nectar to thirsty man, horse and cow alike.
>
> For a mile the cattle have been hastening, called by the moist, enticing smell of it. Arriving at last at the water's edge the leaders plunge eagerly in, to be urged onward again and again till all the mighty herd is in the pool. Knee deep, belly deep, or buried to their brown and tawny shoulders in the refreshing waters, their hoofs sunk in the cool sand and ooze of the bottom, they drink, or stand with half closed eyes, or move to drink and drink again, blissful, greatly content with relief from the hot and dusty trail.
>
> Early with the herd the cowboys have ridden in and while the ponies drink with muzzle thrust in half way to their eyes, the equally thirsty men dip and drink from the brim of their Stetson hats. Now, in scattered groups around the pool they lounge lazily in the saddle, or dismount to cool and rest themselves and tired horses: resting, but ever watchful, ever mindful of duty to the herd.
>
> Up on the bank a mesquite tree with lacy foliage throws a meager shade. A flock of crows, disturbed from their fishing, caw a raucous protest as they fly away to a grove of cottonwoods up the stream. To the left, a low grass covered hill or mesa cuts the horizon. In the far distance is a mountain, a blue cloud shadow at its base. Over all float the cumulous clouds of a perfect summer day. The trail with its long, hot, weary miles of hardship is forgotten. It is an hour of rest, peace, quiet, while watering the herd.[18]

Again, with the exception of references that fill out his narrative, even though not shown in the painting—ponies drinking with their muzzles thrust halfway to their eyes, for example—Reaugh's narrative accurately points out and describes what is shown. Nothing, however, is said about how he composed all these animals, the three mounted cowboys, the rise immediately behind the herd to the left, and the mesquite tree rising above it all. Yet he did just that: got it all together within an implied and controlling diamond shape. We see that the front corner of the diamond is established with the light colored Longhorn low down and almost in the middle of the painting at the frame. The back corner of the diamond lies

[18]Ibid.

with the mounted cowboys and the mesquite tree. The side corners of the diamond are clearly implied as lying off to the right and left of the herd, as is often the case in seventeenth-century Dutch paintings. How Reaugh came to this sophisticated means of composition is not of first importance. What is of importance is that he employed it and that it functions in our appreciation of his work as being more than mere reporting, more than simple illustration.

The third in the series is titled *Bedding the Herd* (plate 37), and we can imagine the effect on Reaugh's assembled audience as he reads from this text while a guitar plays and the painting glows in specially rigged lights:

> It is the end of a long hot day. Up from the canyon and beaten trail, on ground as level and smooth as may be, the tired cattle are brought to rest. Held loosely, they soon begin to lie down, singly and in little groups at first, then more and more until a few men can hold them while the others ride away to where a thin column of smoke marks the location of cook, chuck wagon and the night's camp. . . .
>
> Meantime, around the herd ride the men of the first guard, pushing in perhaps, some straggling steer, with soft persuasive curse; shaping the herd and making it compact; for men must ride around it all through the darkest night.
>
> The scene is one of peace and wondrous beauty. The sinking sun gilds alike the distant cloud and the present mighty herd with golden glory. The western sky is one vast opal, luminous with tints of pink and purple, gold and olive green, flung high around the nucleus of the departing sun. Soon the colors fade, and the dusk is closing in. Grazing ceases, and slowly and with contented grunts, the last of the herd are dropping to rest. A cow bawls plaintively. From across the herd comes the lulling croon of a cowboy's song.[19]

[19]Ibid.

Here, something of Reaugh's long-standing admiration of Turner comes to expression. In a composition as simple and as mysterious as an early Turner seascape, Reaugh sees a western plain almost as if it were a mysterious moving sea on which a great ship—in this case a solitary bull—shows itself against a flaming, golden iridescent setting of the sun that reveals as it hides the world it lights. But this might be too "fancy" a way to describe what Reaugh took in stride as his "simple" way of making a picture about bedding down a lot of cows and bulls and how it looked when the task was accomplished.

Guarding the Herd (plate 38) is the fourth in the Reaugh series. An excerpt from the descriptive prose text reads as follows:

> At midnight the third guard are awakened, bring in their picketed horses, saddle, mount, and . . . ride off to the herd. . . .
>
> It is a glorious night. The brilliant moon, already past the zenith, as the feathery clouds drift across her face, alternately lights and dims again the peaceful scene. Far as the eye can see are huddled forms of sleeping cattle. Here and there a restless steer gets to his feet, stretches, stands awhile, and lies down on the other side with a sigh of deep content. Down in the canyon the owl still hoots. Out on the prairie the coyote's call, high, keen, staccato, mingles with the desperate note of the great gray wolf. The moonlight, glimmering pale on many polished horns becomes weird and ghostly in the shadow of a passing cloud. But always the never-ceasing watch goes on, as back and forth around the sleeping pilgrims go the guard, themselves at times vague, shadowy forms; not moving silently, but singing or humming as they go, that no nervous steer may be startled by unheralded approach, but rather that the weary herd may be soothed and reassured as on and on the riders sing their lullabies. The cattle are in a strange country, far from their native range, and the now familiar presence of the men gives them a feeling of safety.
>
> Two o'clock and "all's well." The air of advancing night grows

crisp and cool. Occasionally there is a stirring of the breeze. A little oftener, perhaps, the cloud shadows sweep across the plain, but the sleeping herd is quiet.[20]

Everything mentioned here, except what could never be shown, like the hooting of the owl, the coyote's call, and the "desperate note of the great gray wolf," is presented to us in this velvety dark, peaceful vision. And we should remember that Reaugh's words come *after* the painting, not *before*. Reaugh is looking at his painting and talking this way even as we look at the same painting more than a half-century later and say, maybe, many of the same things. But unlike Reaugh, who created this vision for us and knows how he did it, we are left with only some evidences: how with his lightest, most brilliant pastels, he created convincing illusions of moonlit clouds in the upper right and in the far left and, in darker colors, a ghostly steer standing at almost dead center reflecting that light. These three lighted-up areas create the corners of an implied triangle standing transparently in the vague space of night with only the shadowed images of cowboys seemingly in control. Every painter from Magnasco to Ryder and from Whistler to Frank Tenney Johnson could well admire this simple means of subjecting a fragment of nature to the constructive and expressive requirements of the artist.

As if these paintings were freeze frames from a film depicting a continuous twenty-four-hour period with a herd of cattle, the next one depicts a *Stampede in the Canyon* (plate 39). The prose, the accompanying "sound track," runs as follows:

Half past two and the boys are counting the minutes before calling the "cocktail guard" that relieves them when a passing cloud causes momentary darkness. A pony stumbled at a badger hole. A slicker becomes loosened, and just at that unfortunate moment a sudden gust of wind whips it from the cowboy's hand to sail with eery outspread wings straight . . . for the very center of the herd. Every wild steer is instantly on his feet. The cowboy's warning shout is too late. The mischief is done. One shiver pulsates through the great huddled mass, then they are tearing down the coulee as only scared cattle can fly, toward the narrowing break that leads to the still narrower canyon below.

Just in front of them are racing the three cowboys, with slack rein and active heel. . . . If they can only keep the lead until the level plains at the mouth of the canyon are reached the herd can be milled and the stampede stopped. They sweep through the break and into the canyon, where the rock walls tower 400 feet overhead. . . .

The canyon awakens and roars and protests with all the power of its echoing lungs; the clashing horns and clattering hoofs answer with increased vigor. Woe and swift death are the lot of anything living that falls under this thundering mass. A steer stumbles, the next one crowds him down, and in shorter time than it takes to fall, the breath is trampled from his body by a hundred hammering hoofs, while a thousand more pelt him into a shapeless mass of hair and blood.

"Only half a mile more, boys, and we're all right," shouts Bill Stewart, and even as he speaks his pony trips and horse and rider are buried under the sea of maddened beasts. As Jack, in a moment of sympathy, impulsively draws rein and slackens his pony, the foremost steer butts it to its knees, and they too, are lost to sight.

So the race goes on, on, on. The remaining guard, with hat off and coat thrown back, is still at the head of the herd, with lips close drawn and the expectancy of swift death on his face. The keen night air is none too cool for his heated blood and he welcomes the life it gives his pony. A short half mile and as the canyon debouches onto the falda and comparatively level ground the cowboy swings his horse to one side and allows the leading steer to come abreast, when from his leveled pistol he sends a belching stream of fire scarce three inches in front of the wild eyes. With a sudden snort and spring that animal swerves to one side; quick as

[20] Ibid.

lightning the pistol is there again and the flashing fire compels him to make a wide circle and finally turn back into the tail of the herd that is just emerging from the canyon.

Close on his heels are the rest of the herd, crowding, bewildered and confused, a wildly whirling maelstrom of milling cattle.[21]

This, the most dramatic painting Reaugh is known to have made, is constructed, whether consciously or not, in a way that makes use of a sophisticated compositional strategy. With all Reaugh's talk about the pictured subject matter, he mentions nothing about how he brought it all together—nothing about how he presented this wild event in terms of a highly organized and expressive design. But his means are there for us to see. Thinking of the cowboy as hero of this event, he places the mounted moonlighted one in lateral dead center. To support and strengthen the role of the cowboy, he paints him at the intersection of two long diagonal directions. One runs from upper right, down along the top of the canyon wall, through the centered cowboy and on to the lower left. The other runs from the upper left of the painting, down along the lighted edge of the slope in the middle distance, through the dark mass of the stampeding cattle, through the cowboy and out along a lighted area of the canyon floor. With all the illusions of light and movement that Reaugh achieves in this work, with all the details of stumbling cattle and a trampled cowboy, it is this compositional X that functions crucially to make this incident more than a candid photographic shot—a work of art.

The sixth painting, *Milling Cattle* (plate 40), depicts the situation on the plains as the stampeding cattle gradually quiet down. The prose narrative used in conjunction with it provides the bridge between *Stampede in the Canyon* and the seventh and last painting in the series. The text used in connection with *Milling Cattle* reads as follows:

[21]Ibid.

All through the gray morning watch the one cowboy on weary trembling horse rides just without the whirling circle of the frantic milling herd. The mad pace grows slower at last, but it seems long hours before, through the frenzied bellowing and the roar and rattle of hoofs and horn came the welcome shouts of other men. Then he can withdraw a little to one side and rest his drooping horse.

The soft, sweet breath of dawn sweeps over the western plains. The prairie sparrow twitters sleepy to its mate. The sky grows eloquent of coming day. Long lances of light shoot up to the zenith and presently the sun breaks thru its veil of cloud and glints and glistens on the rocky crowns of the hills and tips with rosy light the mighty dust cloud that rises from the valley.

The pace of the milling cattle grows even slower until at last it is controlled. The milling ceases. The stampede is stopped.

Up in the silent canyon, so lately filled with uproarious life, lie seventy-three dead cattle and two horses and cowboys crushed into unrecognizable shapes.

A meadow lark sings. The sparrow's twitter becomes a hymn of ecstasy and praise. The cottonwood trembles and whispers in the morning breeze and breaks into glory in the morning sun, but they in the canyon have passed beyond its narrow limits to the grander heights and fairer plains across the great divide.[22]

With his *Milling Cattle*, Reaugh diminishes the role of the herd, relegating it to a relatively small shadowed area to the left and bottom of the painting. Here, Reaugh appears more concerned with expressing the camaraderie, the bond that necessarily exists between cowboys on the trail. Across a great pictorial distance he has a lone cowboy wave to two others high on a bluff who have come to take the next watch. Against the "long lances of light" heralding dawn, they stand ready to ride on down and close the distance. Is it only the tell-tale waving of the cowboy in the foreground that establishes this bond? Not

[22]Ibid.

really. It is also the long curving edge of the slope that runs through him and his mount and up to the tableland where the other cowboys announce their expected arrival—a strictly compositional device that ties these men together across the wild open space.

The seventh and last painting of the series, *The Herd Moves On* (plate 41), echoes the first: the passage of the twenty-four hours with the herd brings us back, not to the same landscape, but to the beginning of another day on the trail. "It is late forenoon," the accompanying text reads,

> the plains glow with the light of midday sun. The air quivers with the growing heat. Far as the eye can see the ground is covered with gray brown sage grass or the golden yellow of curly mesquite. In the distance the herd, quieted again, moves on under its canopy of dust. The delayed chuck wagon is still in the rear. Further and to the left is a thin gray line of mesquites, and on the far horizon is a low blue range of hills.
>
> Back at the canyon quiet settles over the plain. A meadow lark sings. Overhead turkey buzzards are circling. A coyote slinks down from the breaks. Down in the canyon, at the heads of new graves are two flat rocks, and in uncertain letters, rudely carved with a cowboy's knife, on one is "Bill Stewart," on the other "Jack."
>
> In the left foreground of the picture a lone cowboy is riding to overtake the outfit. Yesterday's work is ended. Another day's work has begun, as the herd moves on.[23]

This almost pure landscape, with two-thirds of its area given over to a sun-saturated sky, comes the closest of this series to being an impressionist painting. With so little to describe about the herd, except that it has moved on under "a canopy of dust," with only one diminutive cowboy hurrying to catch up and only a tiny light spot that stands for the distant chuck wagon, Reaugh is free to invest this painting with what, all along, may have been closest to his heart—the light, atmosphere, and illimitable space of the open plains.

Reaugh's choice of pastel as his principal medium was not fortuitous. Besides being well adapted to transport and use in open country—small and light, and with no required turpentine, oils, varnishes, or brushes—pastel, by its very nature, easily lends itself to creating subtle atmospheric effects. And more than that, sticks of pastel can be sharpened to produce fine lines and sharp contours; witness the fine detail possible in Reaugh's pastel paintings that measure only a few square inches. Reaugh knew all this and he saw how the master, La Tour, had made use of it.

In the pamphlet *Pastel*, Reaugh says: "The effective field of pastel as a medium lies somewhat between those of oil and watercolor; giving the delicacy of the one or the depth and vigor of the other, with some excellent qualities all its own. No other medium can so truthfully give the freshness and bloom of childhood complexion, or the feeling of air in landscape. . . ." Further on he speaks of getting "the best atmospheric effects" and "where a color can be made by combining several contrasting colors (as red, blue and yellow, or even simply red and green) the resulting color will be more live, vibratory and atmospheric than if made with a single pastel of the desired color," and "a sketch from nature . . . should be a study of a definite time and place and a reliable work of reference."[24]

Reaugh used pastels almost exclusively for his work done directly from nature. These on-the-spot, vibrant studies are the principal basis for all his larger, more sustained works in pastels and in oils. Different from most other Western painters of the time, this technique is how Reaugh brought the light and atmosphere, as well as the subject matter, of the plains

[23] Ibid.

[24] Reaugh, *Pastel*.

country to the paintings we recognize today as distinctively his. And this is true whether he closes in on a group of thistles (plate 4) or some cardinal flowers (plate 9) or opens up to a vision such as his *Singing Shepherd of Acoma* (plate 8).

There is no questioning that Frank Reaugh was our first and preeminent painter of the Longhorn—he even said as much. However, just to recognize that his principal subject was that great animal is not to do full justice to this remarkable artist. It is important that we recognize not only *what* Reaugh painted, but *how* he painted. In all but his most fragmentary studies—really notes to himself concerning the anatomy and typical positions of the Longhorn—he sketched and painted the animal as alive *in nature*. He researched and recorded the Longhorn in its natural habitat on the western plains under western skies. He sat out there with his lap easel, folding stool, umbrella, and pastels in the same changing light and atmosphere as the subjects he painted. In an actual way Frank Reaugh shared this common ambience, and he was uncommonly sensitive to its transitory and determinant qualities. His paintings, as well as being moving records of the Longhorn and a passing way of life, are also celebrations of the unifying power of light to define and obscure the objects of this world. In this sense Reaugh was an impressionist painter.

Much of the lyrical nostalgia we often experience when looking at a Reaugh painting is induced by the power of the painting to create in us an image of ideal harmony. True, there stands the bull looking straight at us, the others behind, the grass rolling away toward the distant horizon (plate 6); but all this is brought under the influence of a sky radiating a particular quality of light through the dusty or clear, morning or afternoon atmosphere. And every color in the grass, in the coats of the animals, and on the plain beyond is brought into this vision of harmony by mixing the colors of the prevailing light and atmosphere with the colors of every object it touches.

In a deep sense it is more than Longhorns, cowboys, and landscapes that comprise Reaugh's subject matter. Any adequate response to his work must include recognition of the fact that light and atmosphere play a powerful role in themselves as prime subject matter in his paintings. Reaugh did not go as far as Monet or Pissarro, the French nineteenth-century "scientific" impressionists, who sometimes allowed their landscapes to be all but completely dissolved in patterns of the spectrum colors of sunlight and shadow. Reaugh held to the tactile qualities of the animals and places he knew so well, but he also gave palpable form to the elusive but unifying qualities of the immediately prevailing light and atmosphere. This is one of the characteristics that separates so many of Reaugh's paintings from those of Frederic Remington and Charles Russell, his much more famous contemporaries. Both Remington and Russell were largely concerned with the life, customs, and actions of cowboys and Indians in settings of sky and ground that function more as stage props than as crucial determinants. Often they presented their subject matter in anecdotal terms, sometimes with the humorous intent of well-drawn cartoons. Next to nothing of this sort appears in the work of Frank Reaugh.

This writer will leave it to others to determine and evaluate Frank Reaugh's place in the historical context of American art. That he has a significant place there this writer has no doubt—and he has no doubt, either, that subsequent studies of the man and his work will rescue both from the relative anonymity that Frank Reaugh's modesty and happy satisfaction with his provincial Texas life have so long encouraged.

Artists come first: they create the art. Historians and critics of art must necessarily follow, but not so far behind as they have in the case of Frank Reaugh. Perhaps the most generous attitude we can assume toward those straggler historian-critics is suggested by J. Evetts Haley in his essay *F. Reaugh—Man and*

Artist: "Among the great artists of the frontier who caught the challenge and the glory of that vital age in enduring color, the name of Frank Reaugh is now rarely mentioned. But when we consider the wide range of action, and the vivid and almost infinite variety of subject matter that invited attention, it is not altogether surprising that historians and critics have sometimes ridden laggard horses."[25]

Donald L. Weismann

[25] J. Evetts Haley, *F. Reaugh—Man and Artist* (El Paso: Carl Hertzog, 1960).

PLATE 1

Sketch for Watering the Herd, 1887

Pastel

3 ¼ × 6

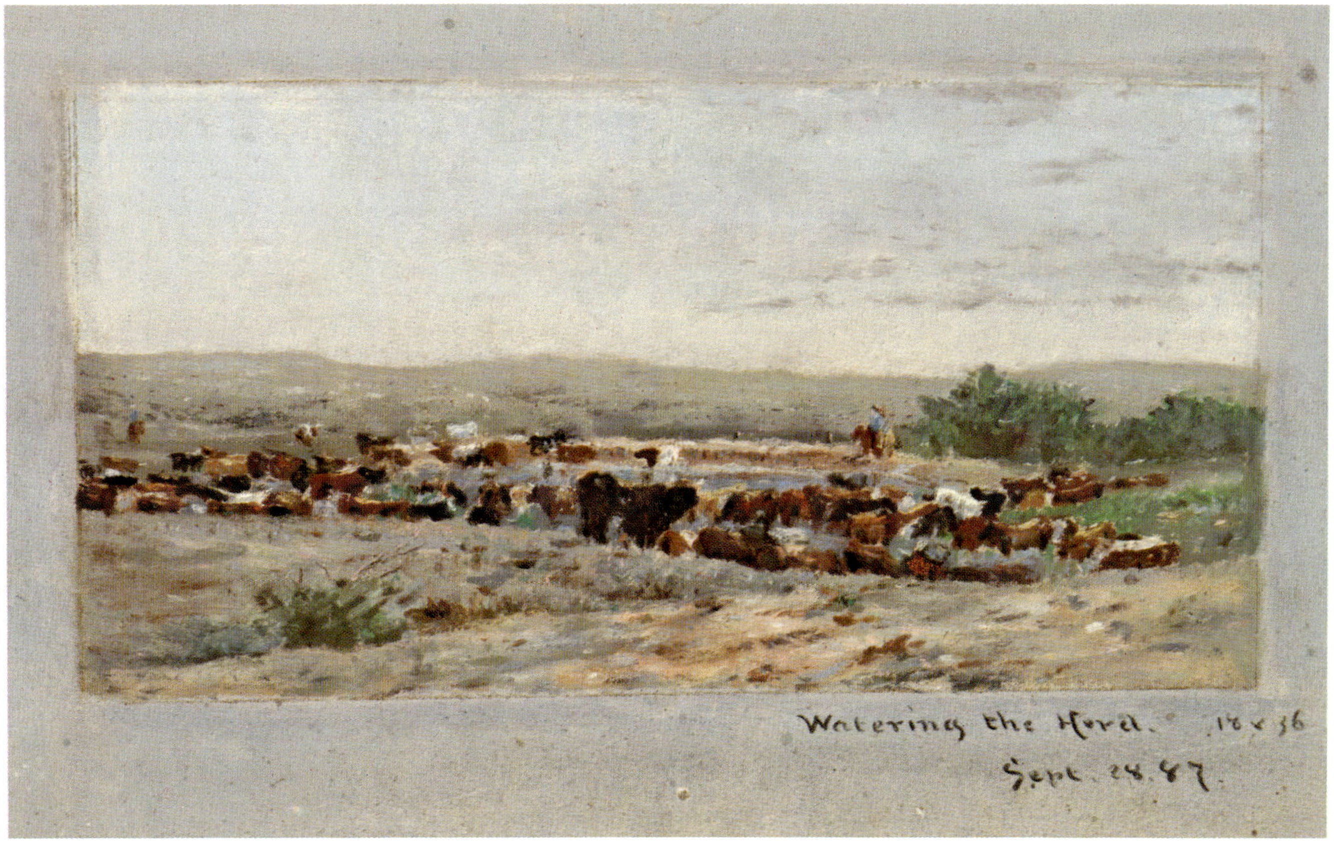
Watering the Herd. 18 x 36
Sept. 28. 87.

PLATE 2

Watering the Herd, 1889

Oil

18 × 34

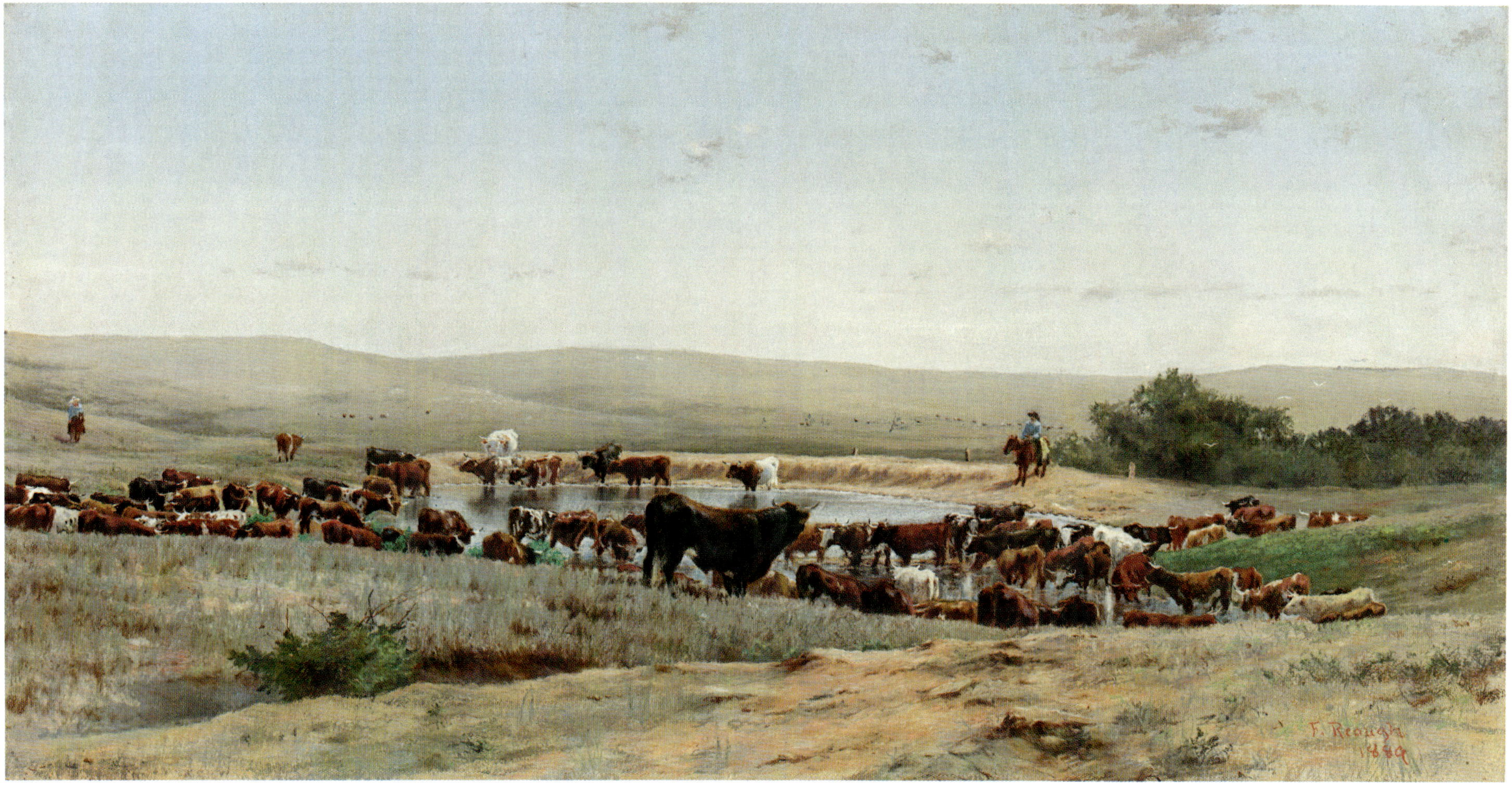
F. Reaugh
1889

PLATE 3
Powder River
Oil
19¾ × 39⅜

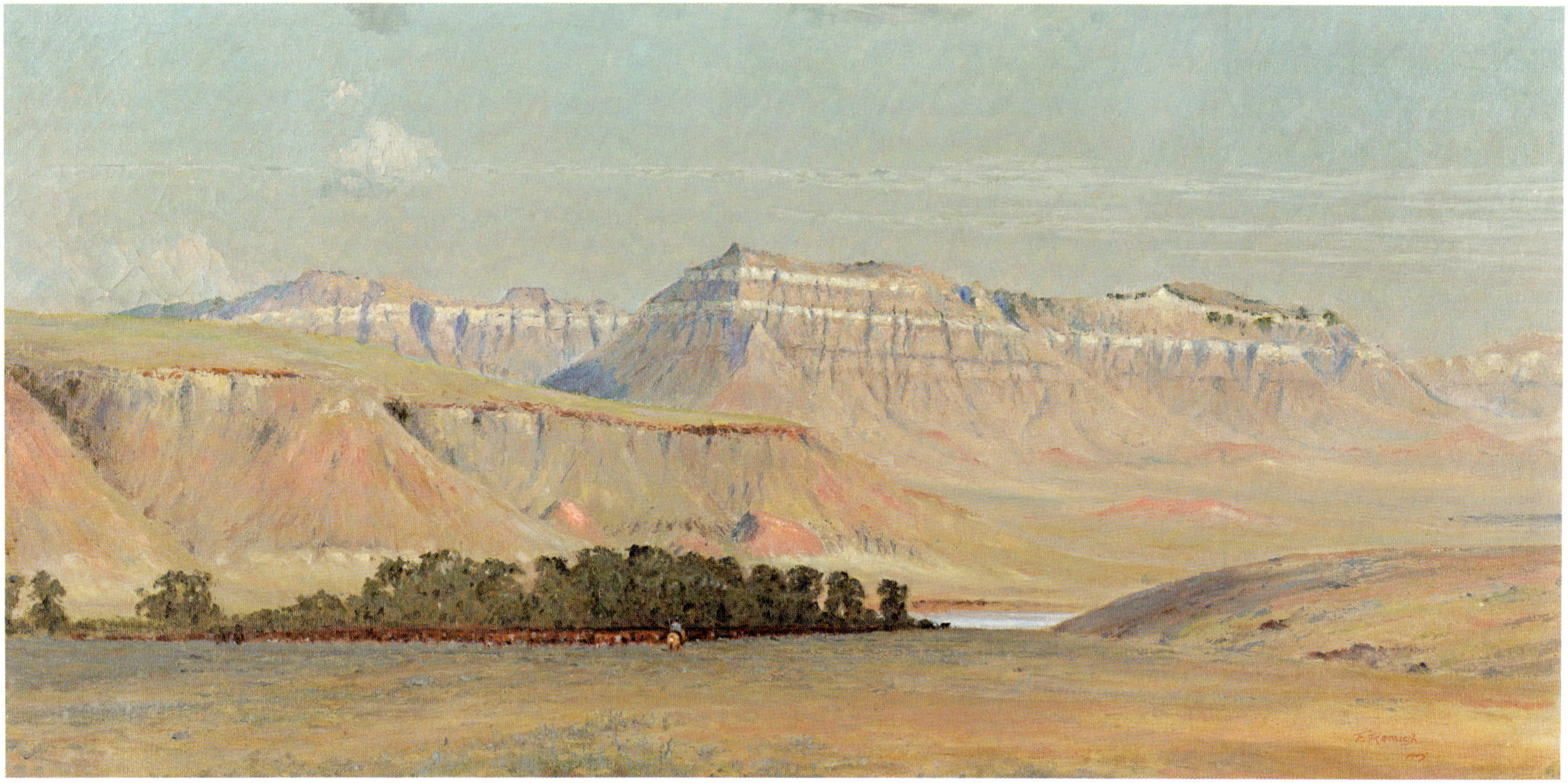

Plate 4

Purple Thistles

Pastel

$7 \times 3\frac{1}{2}$

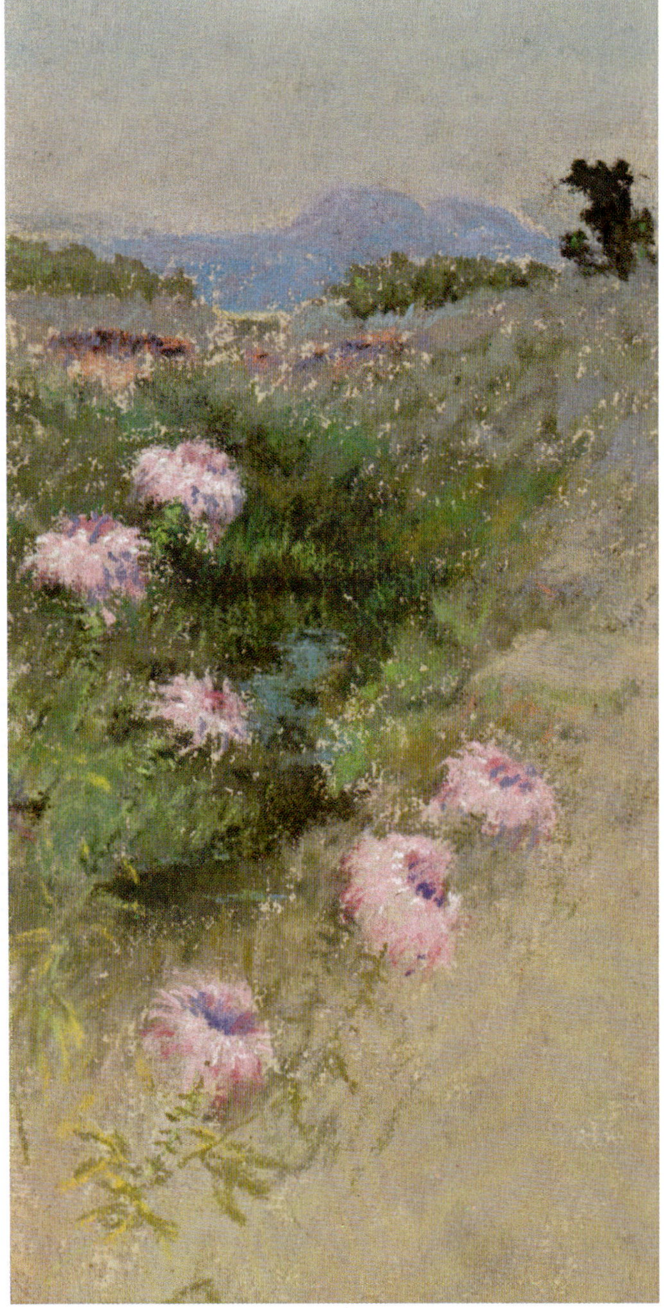

PLATE 5

Morning Light

Pastel

16 × 9

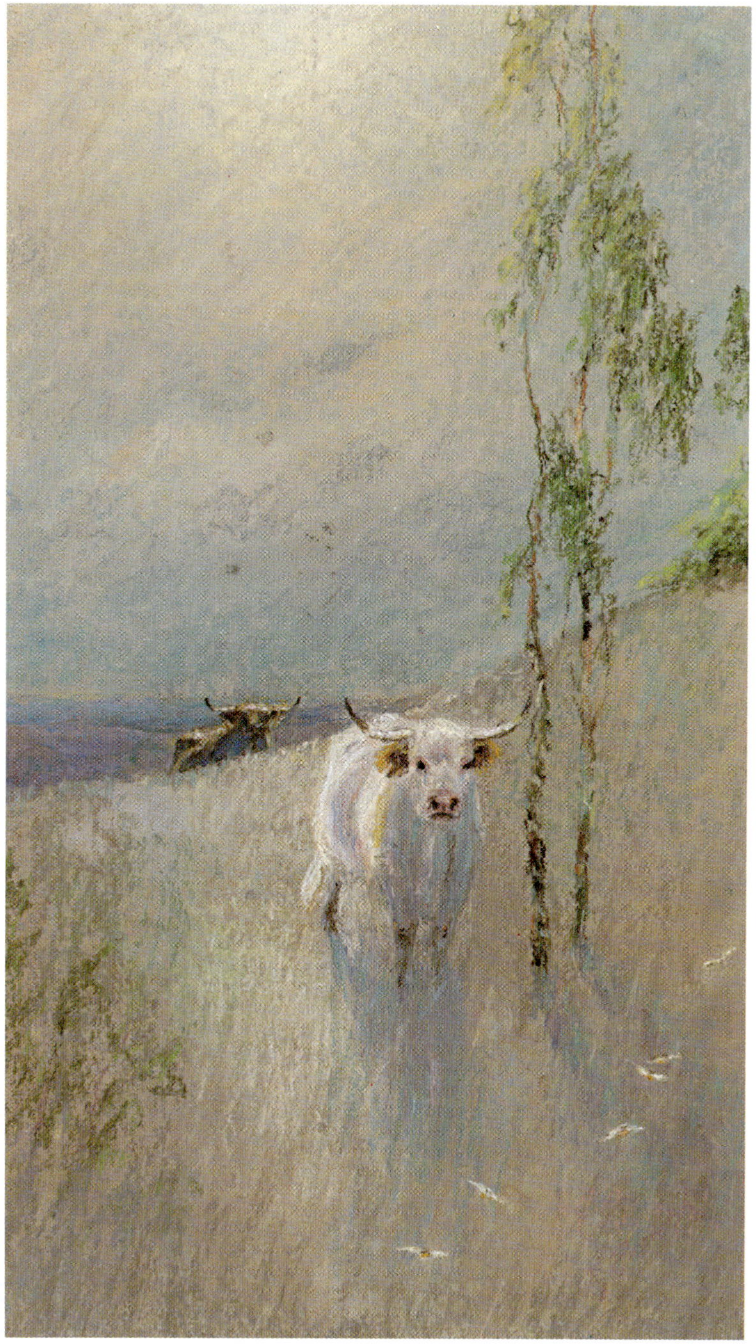

PLATE 6

Approaching Herd

Oil

24 × 48

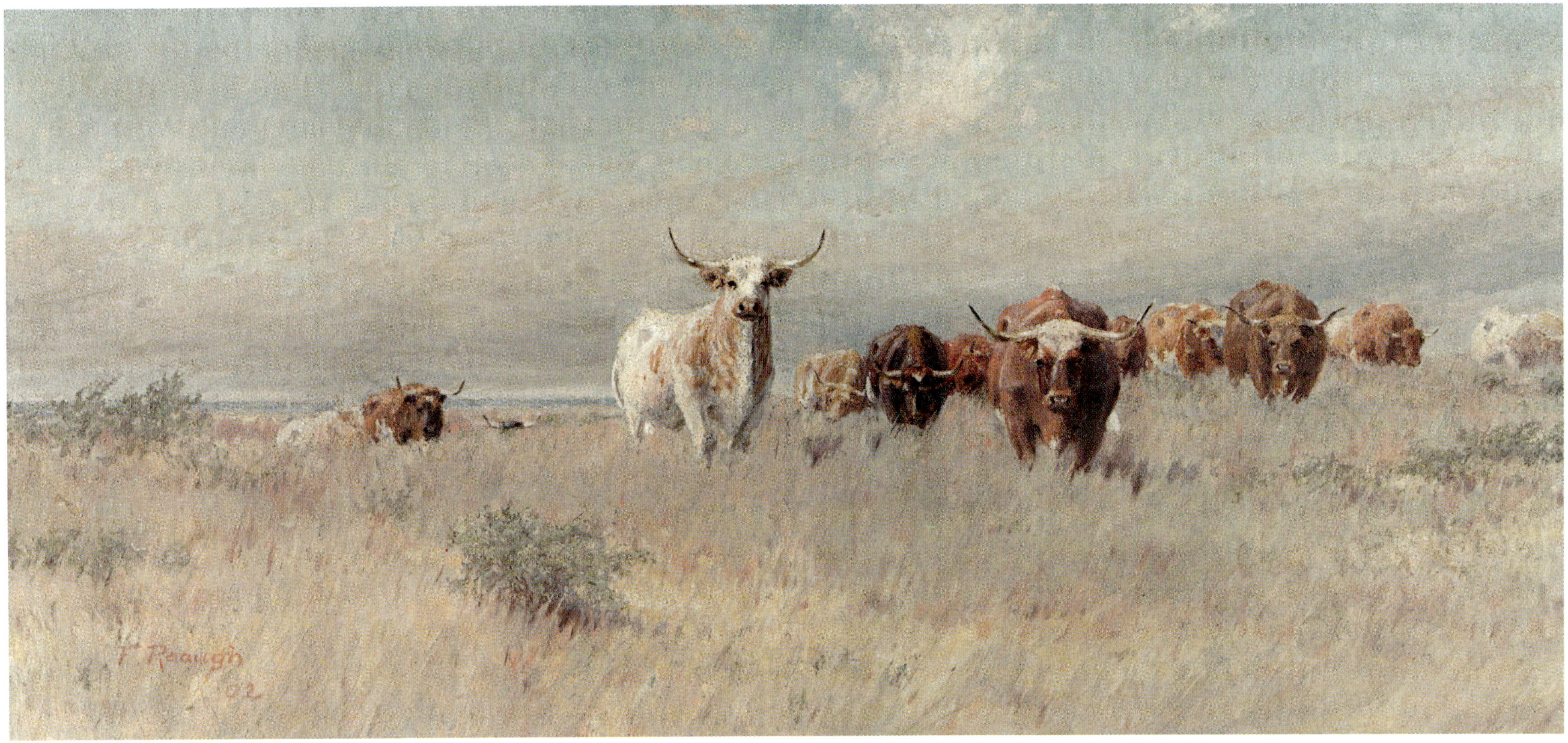
F. Reaugh
'02

PLATE 7

Double Mountain

Oil

14 × 30

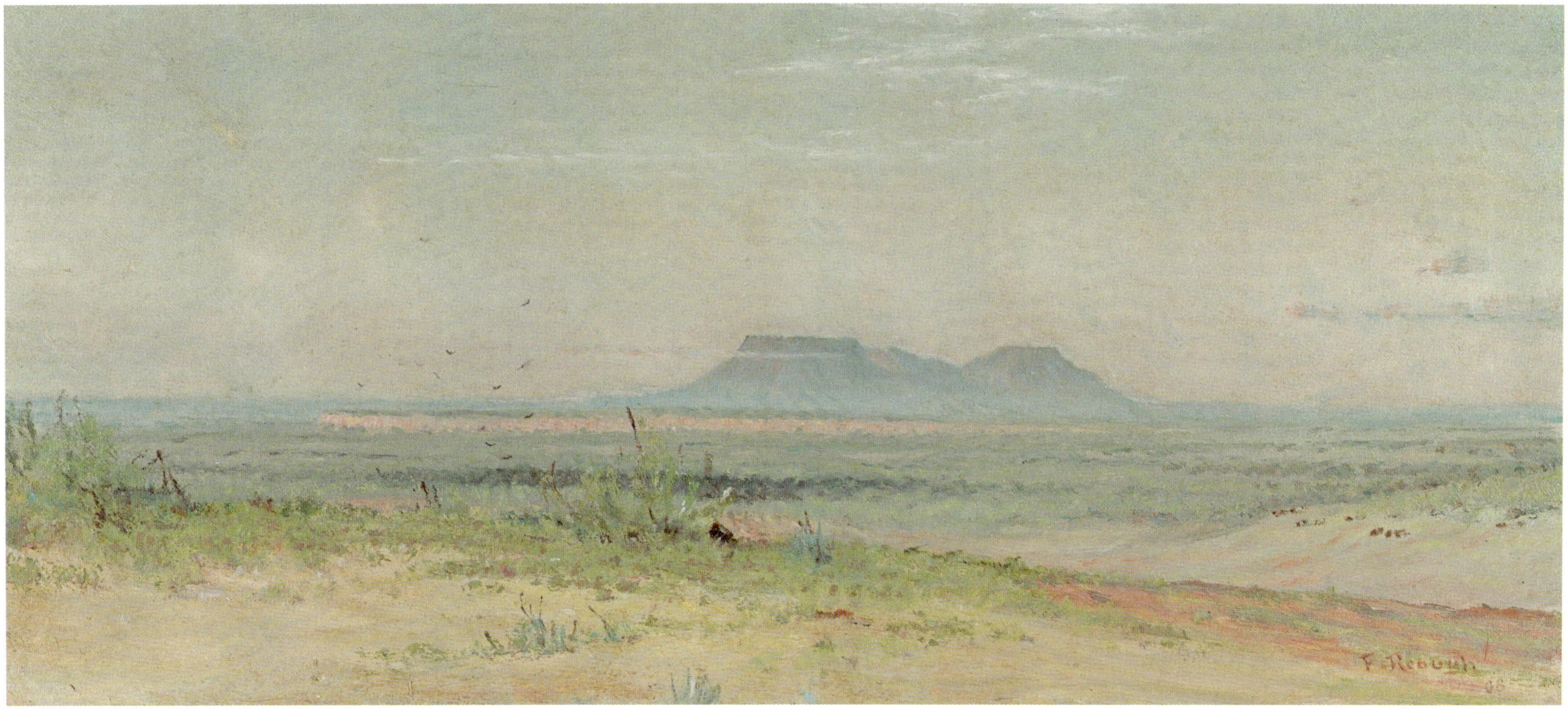

PLATE 8

The Singing Shepherd of Acoma

Pastel

39 1/4 × 19 1/2

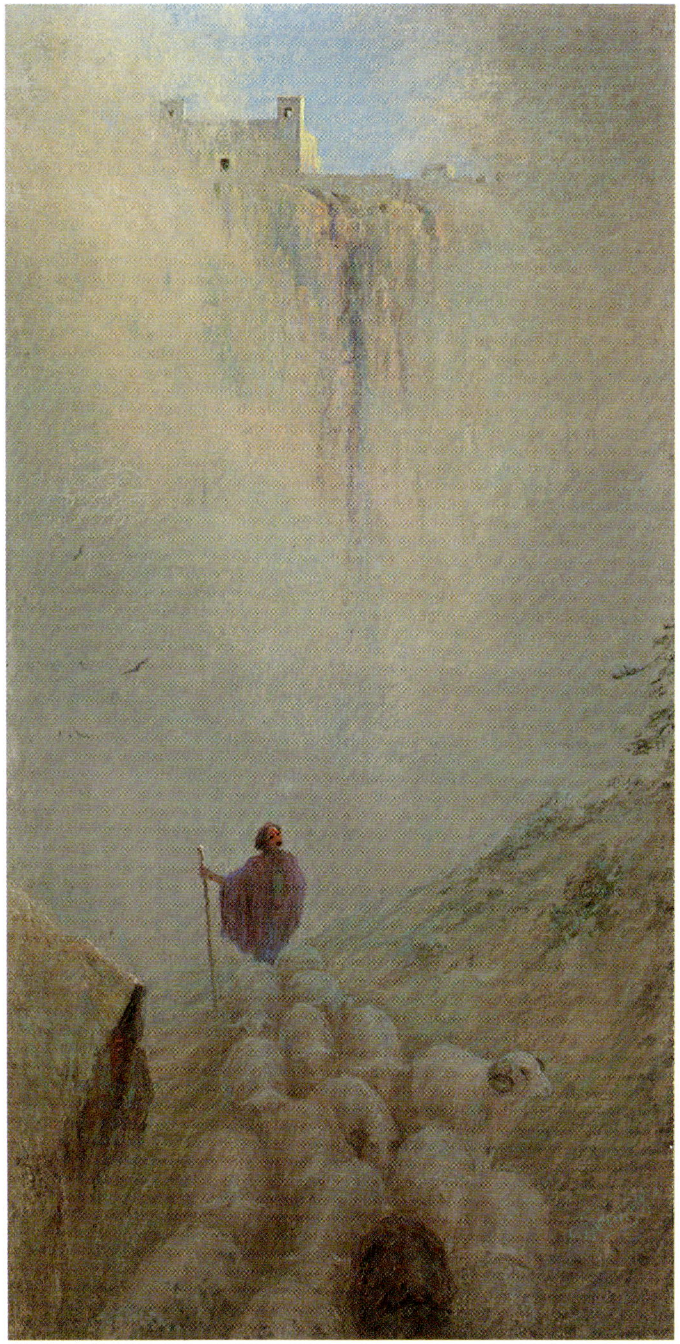

Plate 9

Cardinal Flowers, Devil's River

Pastel

7 × 3 ½

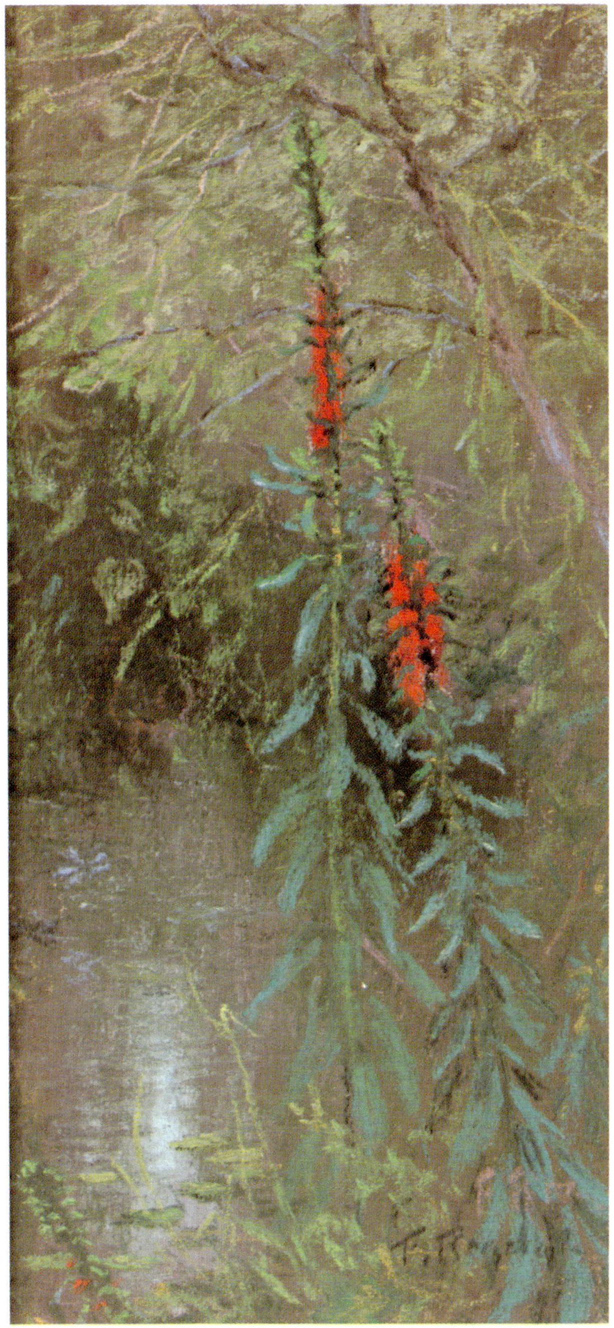

PLATE 10

Cattle in Draw

Pastel

8¾ × 11½

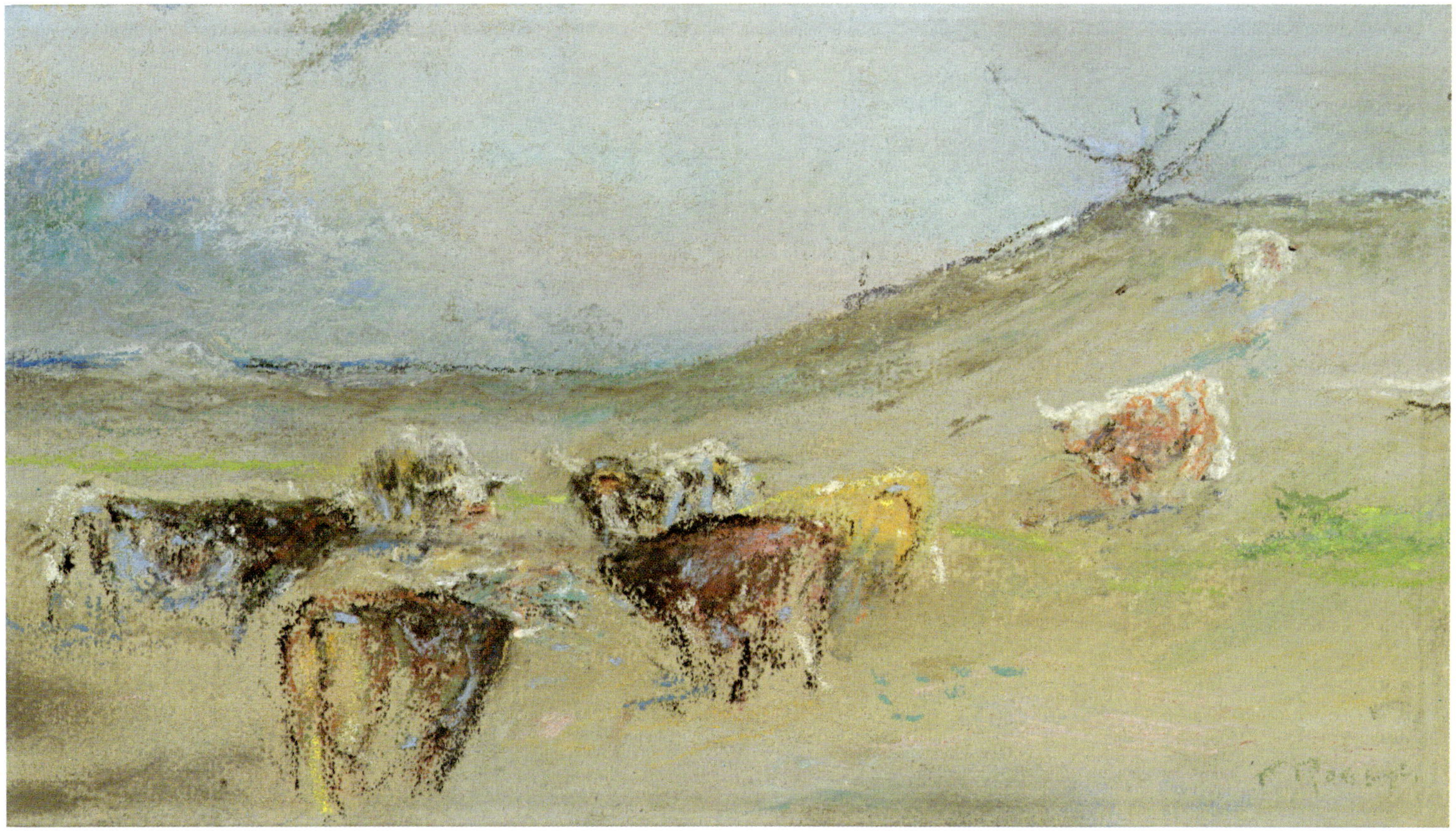

Plate 11

Comanche Peak

Oil

2 ½ × 8

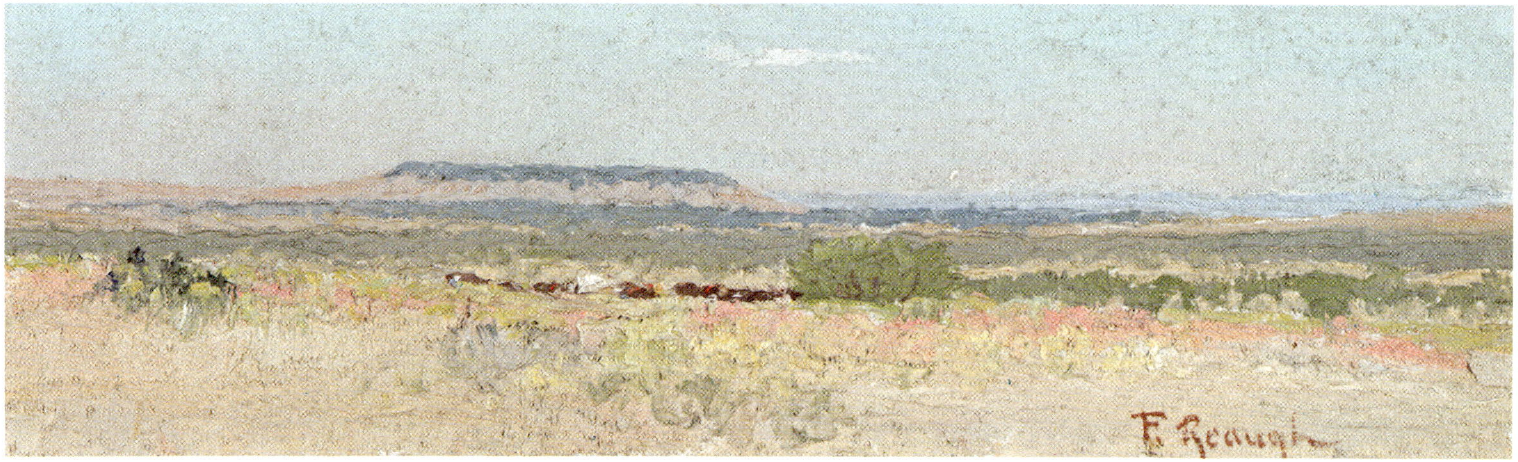
F. Reaugh

PLATE 12

Cattle Looking into Watering Hole

Pastel

3 × 6½

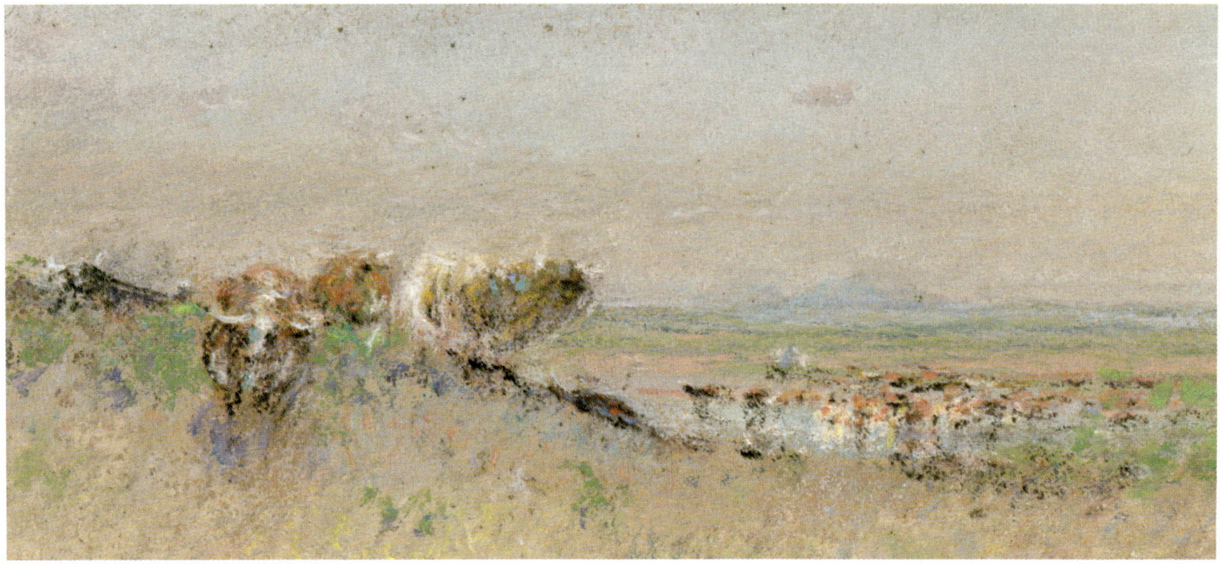

PLATE 13

Cross Timbers Twilight

Pastel

11 × 25¼

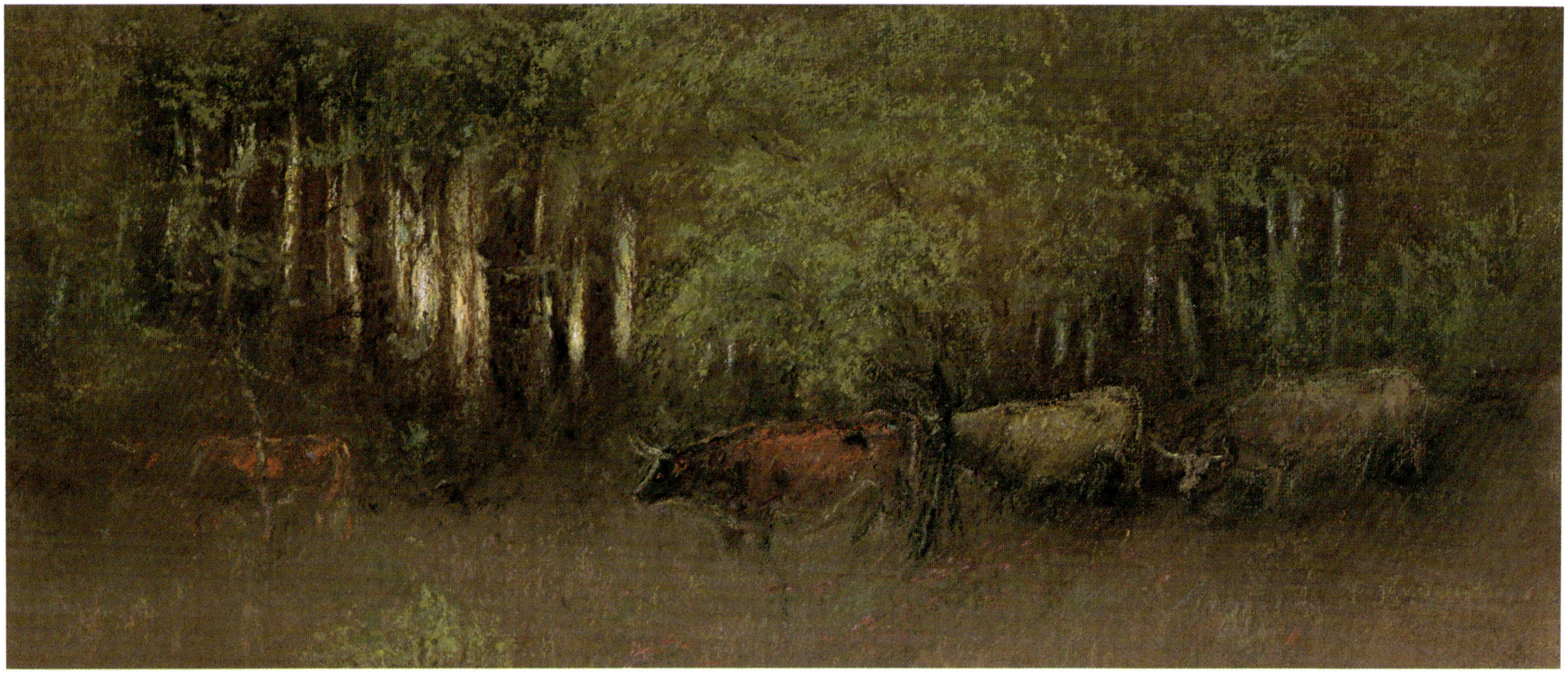

PLATE 14
Organ Mountain
Pastel
3 × 6½

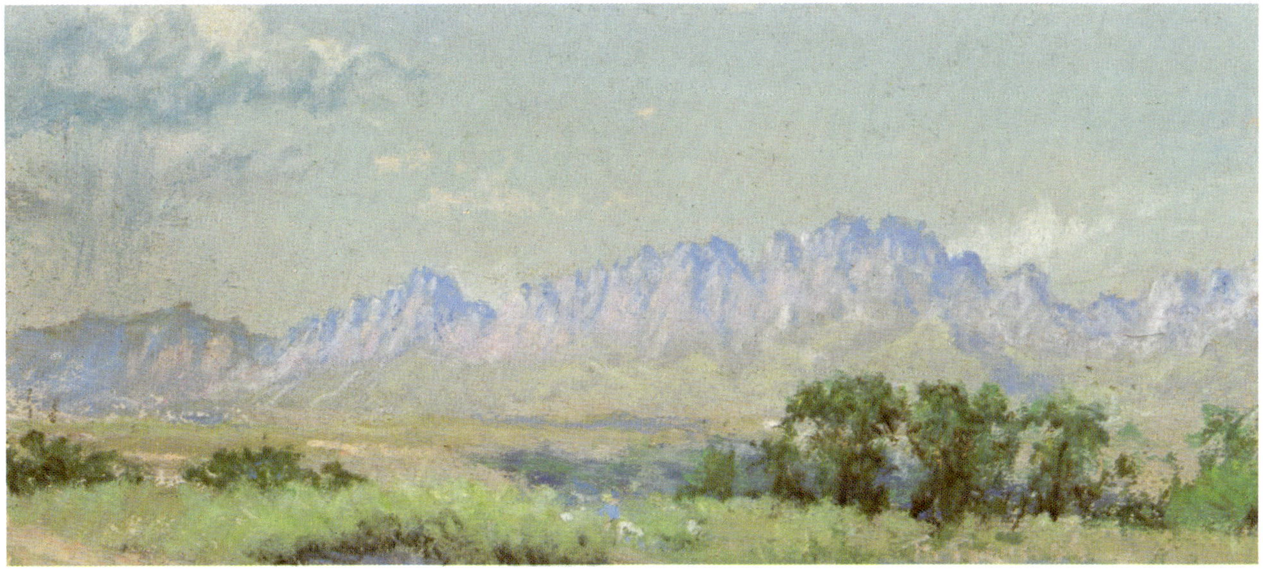

Plate 15

Landscape with Single Cow

Pastel

3 × 6½

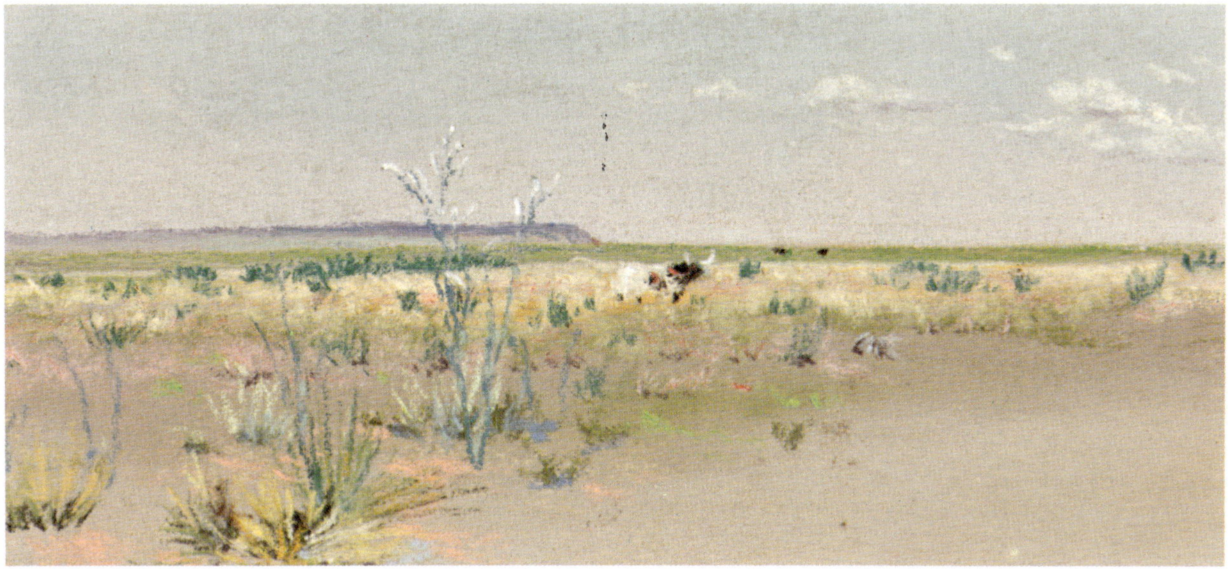

PLATE 16

Lightning

Pastel

$5\frac{3}{4} \times 9$

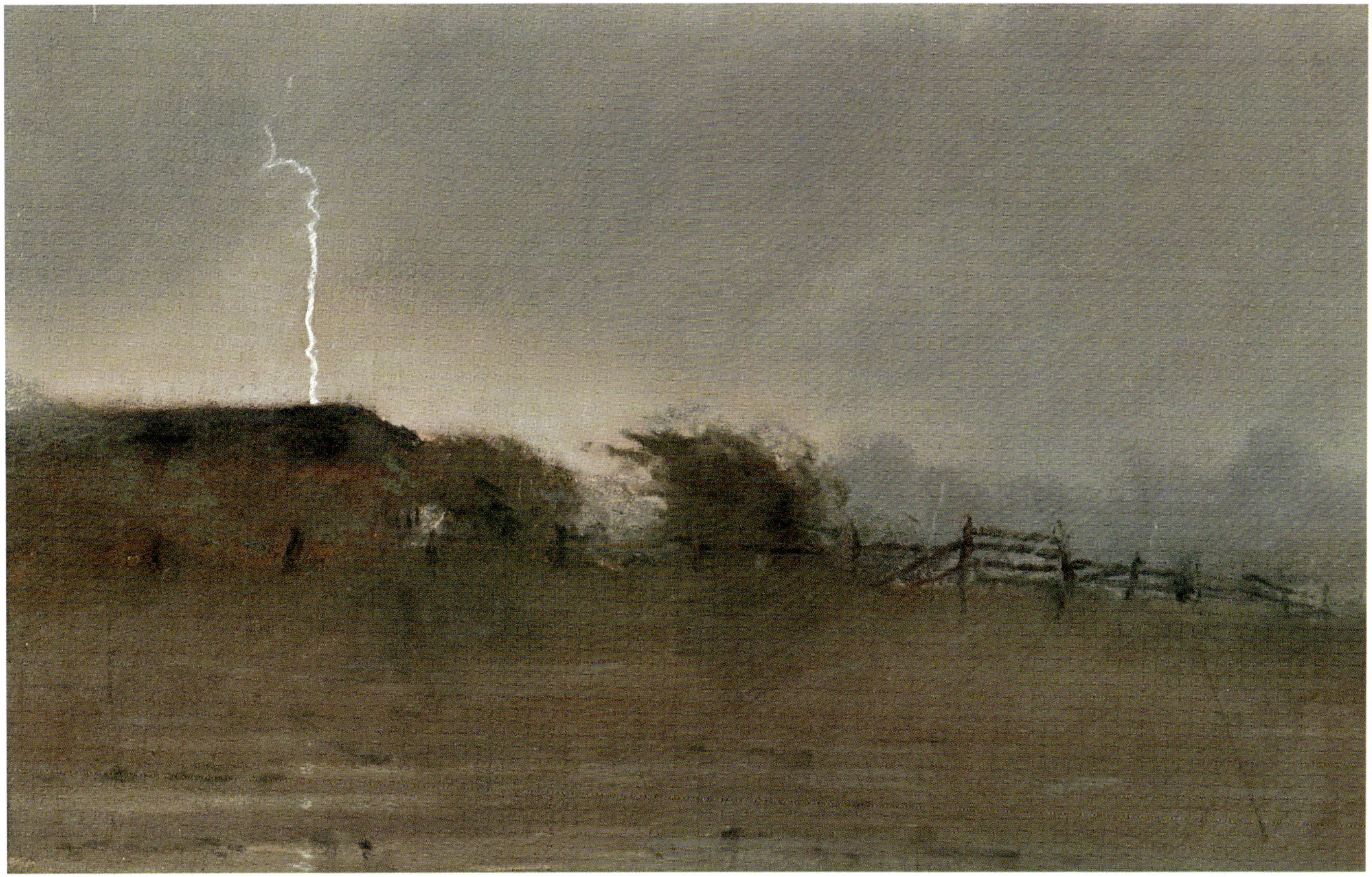

PLATE 17

Landscape with Mesa

Pastel

$3\frac{3}{4} \times 9\frac{1}{4}$

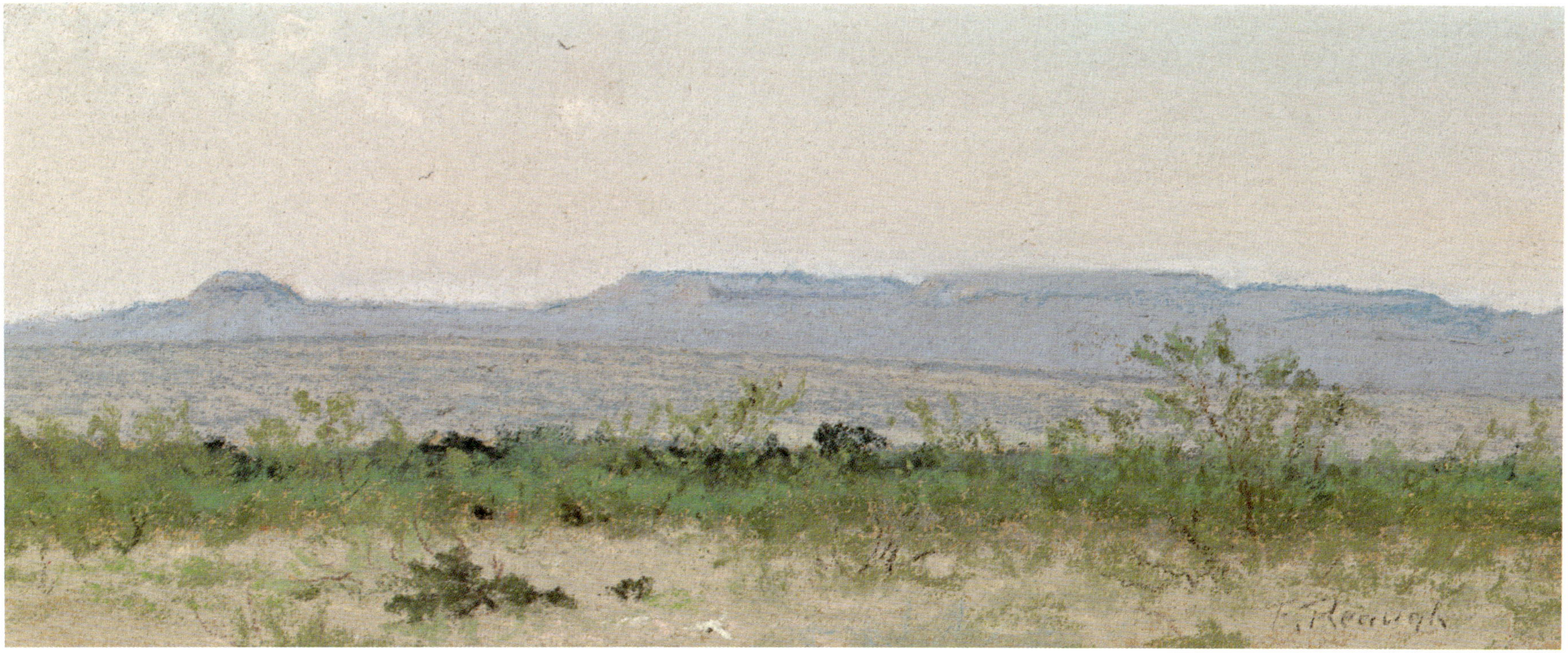

PLATE 18

Coming Herd—Morning

Pastel

12 × 24

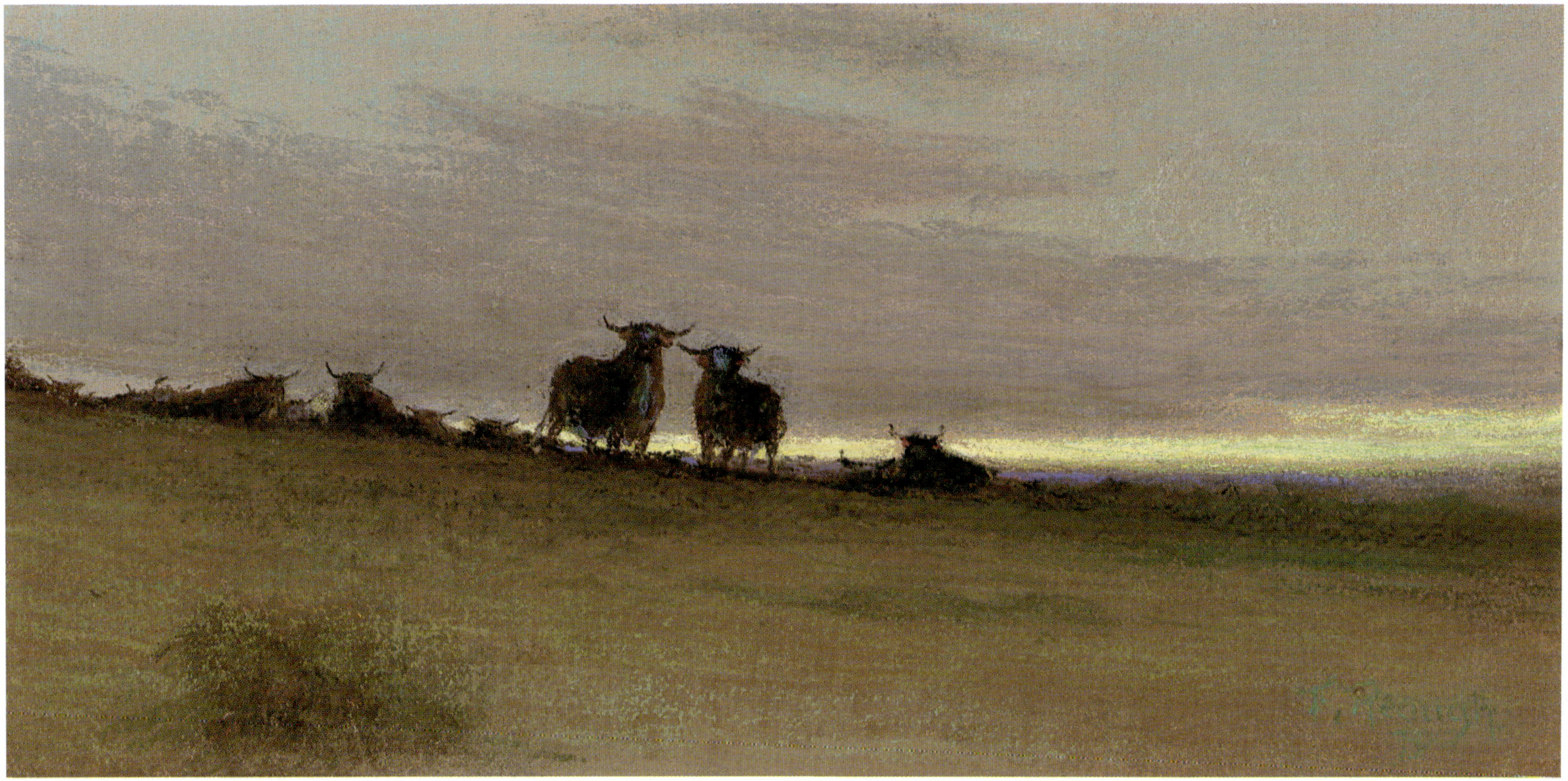

PLATE 19

Landscapes with Steers

Pastel

8 × 6

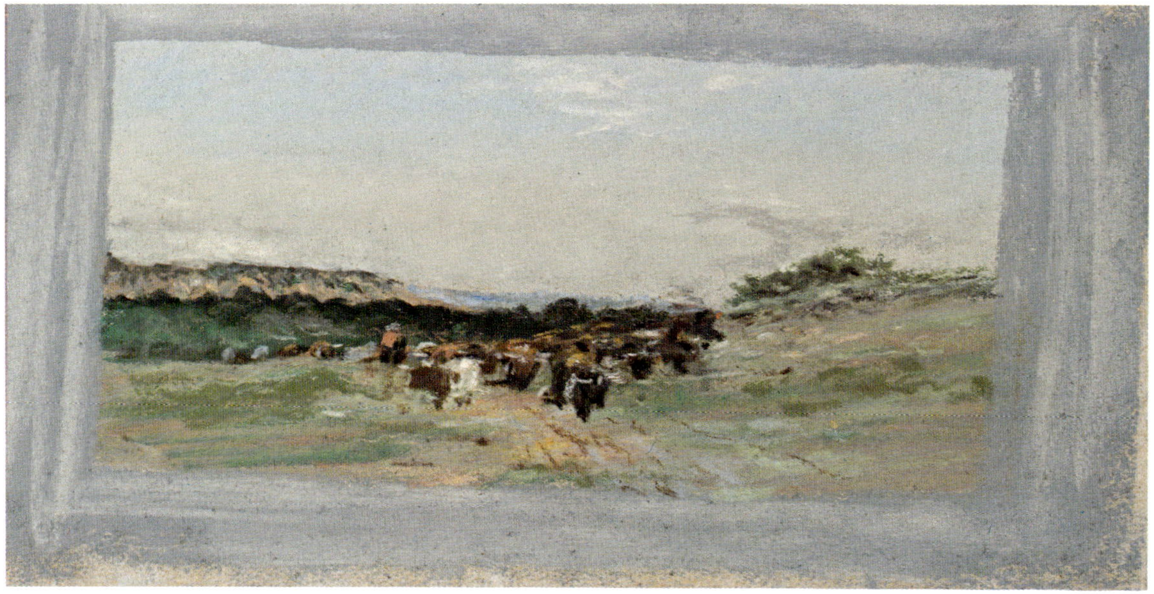

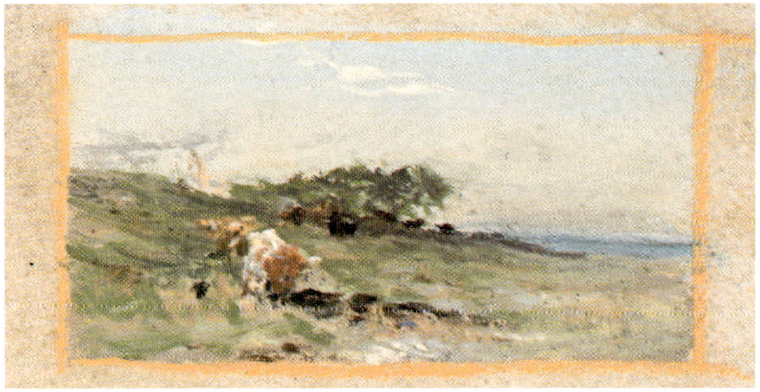

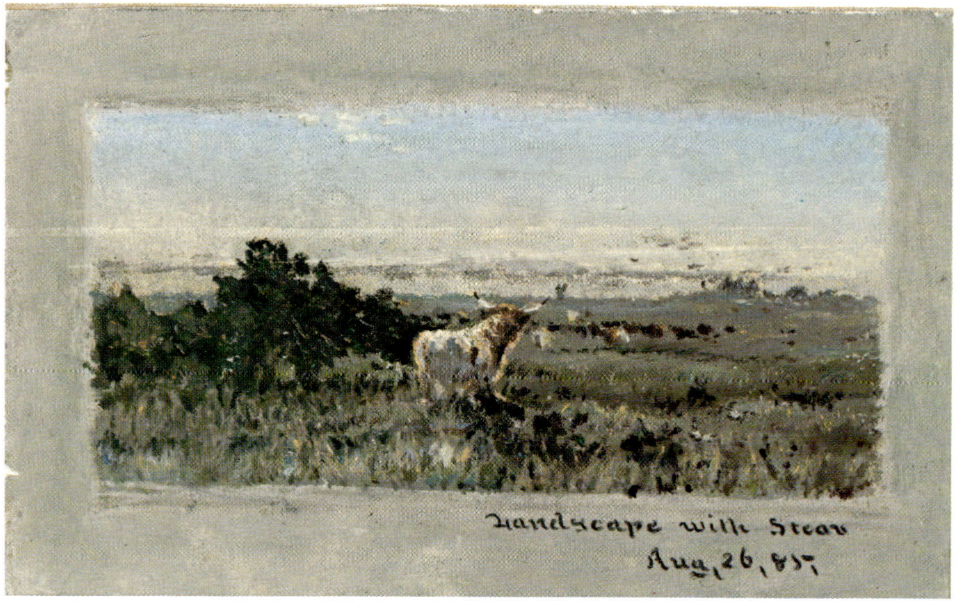
Landscape with Steer
Aug, 26, 85

PLATE 20

Panel of Miniatures

Pastel

9 × 11¾

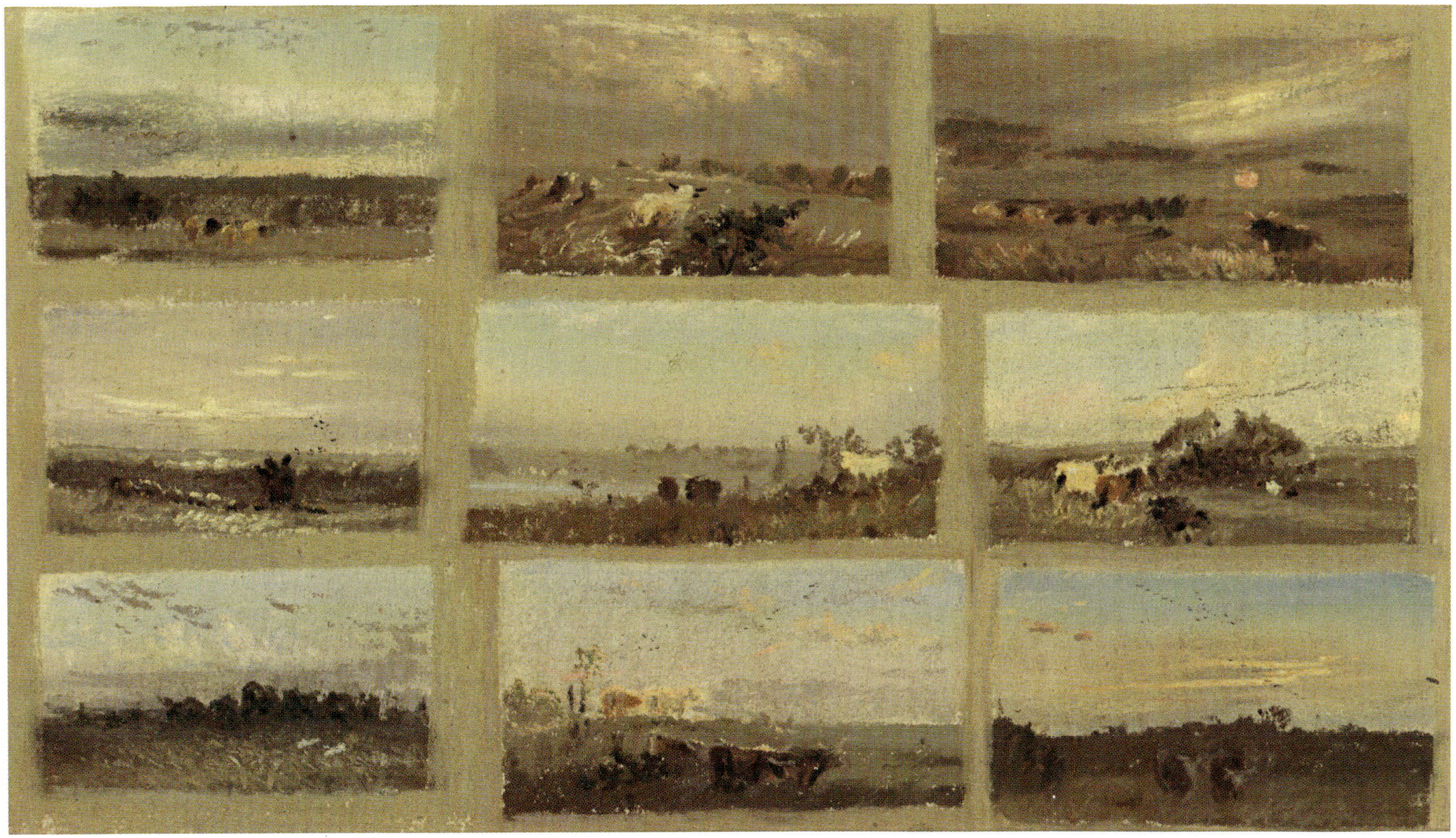

PLATE 21
Cattle Grazing
Pastel
9 × 12½

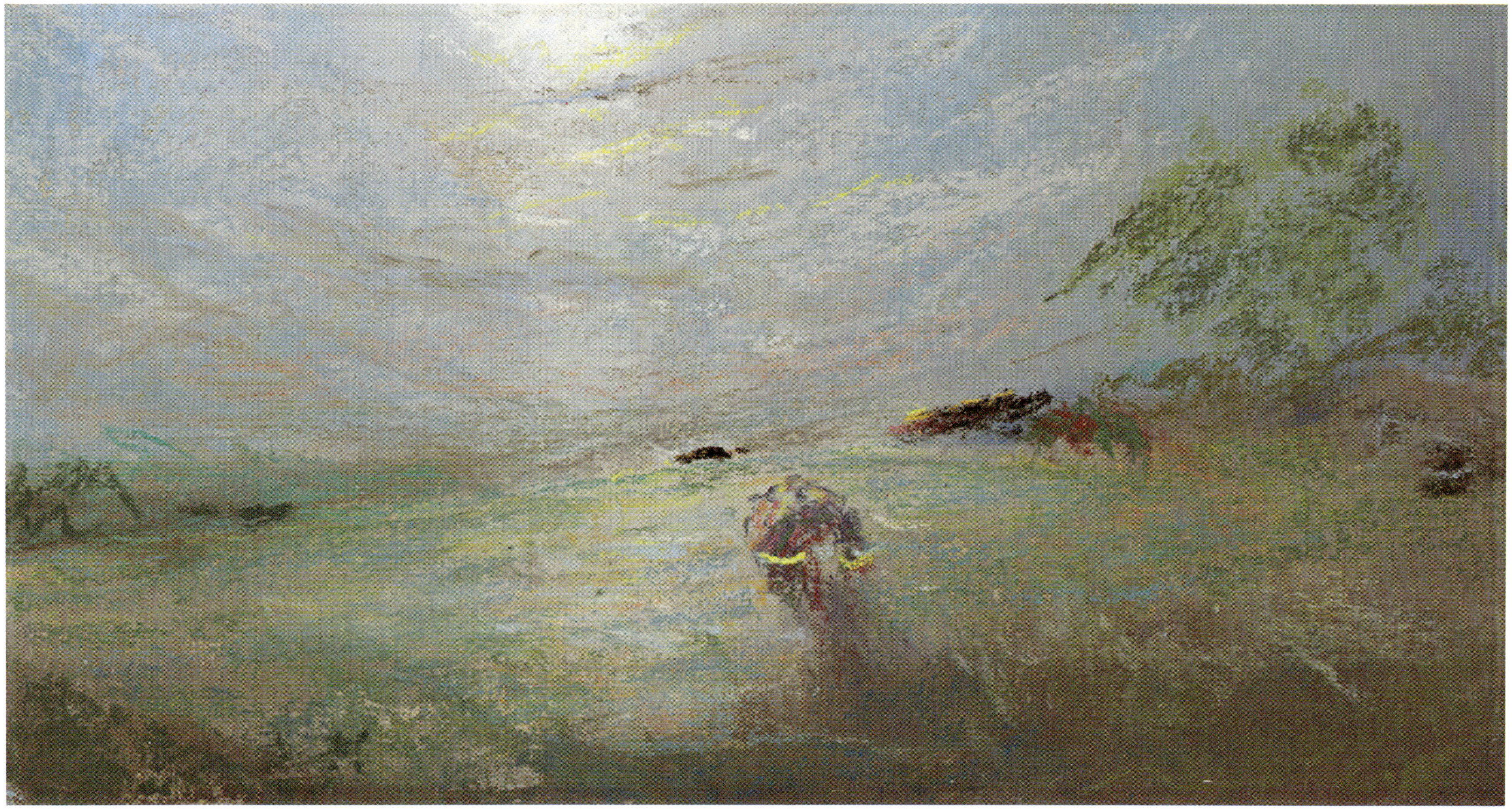

PLATE 22

Detail for Cattle Sketch

Pastel

4 × 9

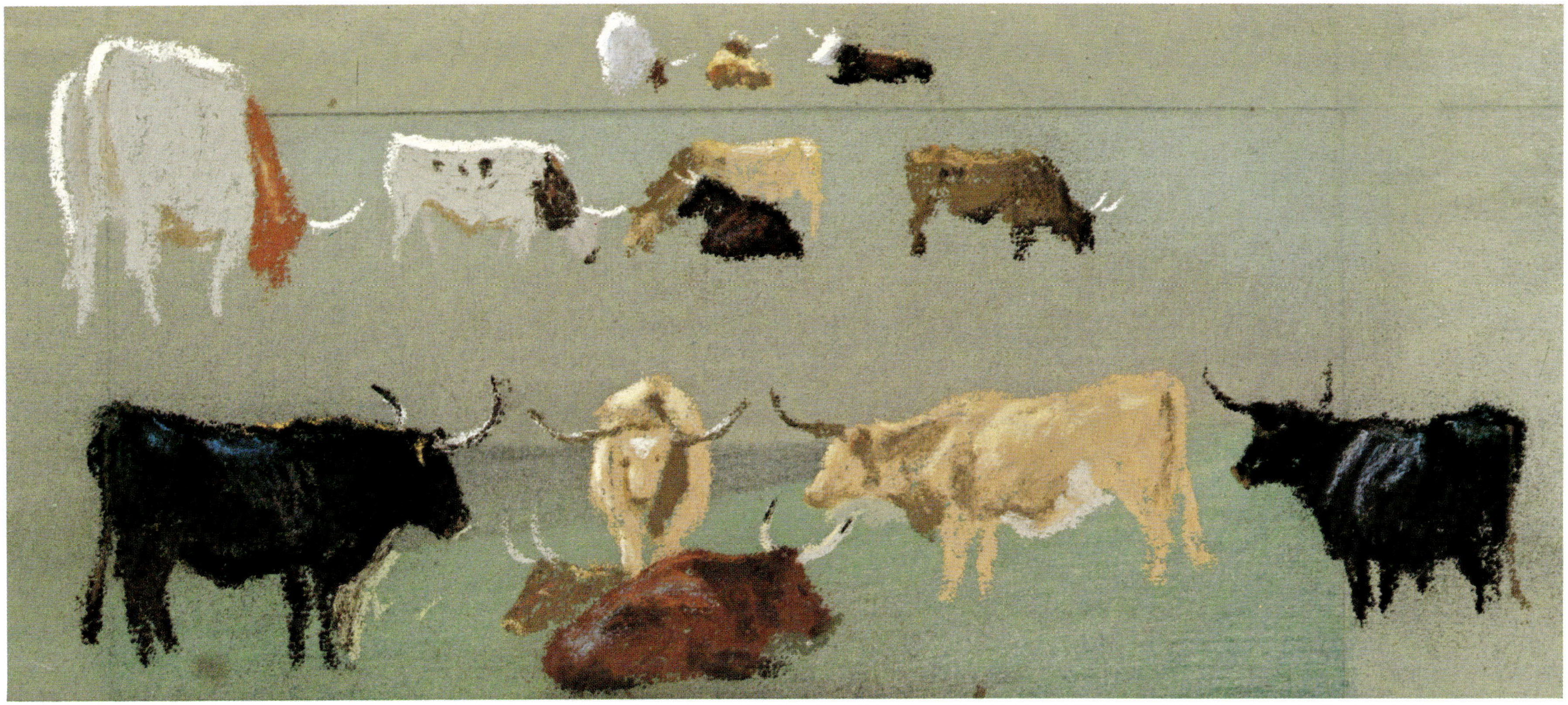

PLATE 23

Cattle over Slope

Pastel

9 1/4 × 13 1/4

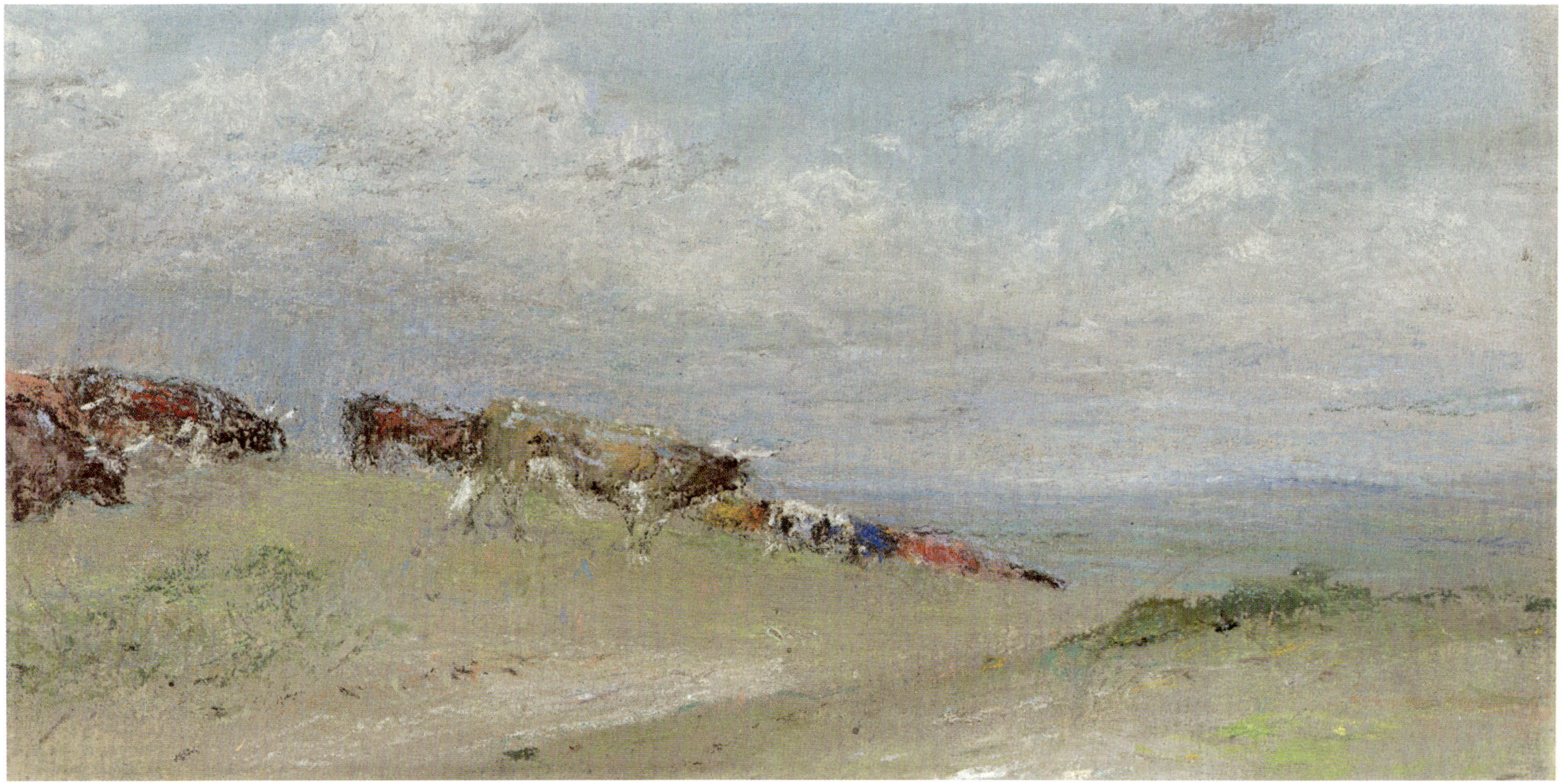

PLATE 24

Afternoon Nap

Pastel

6½ × 7

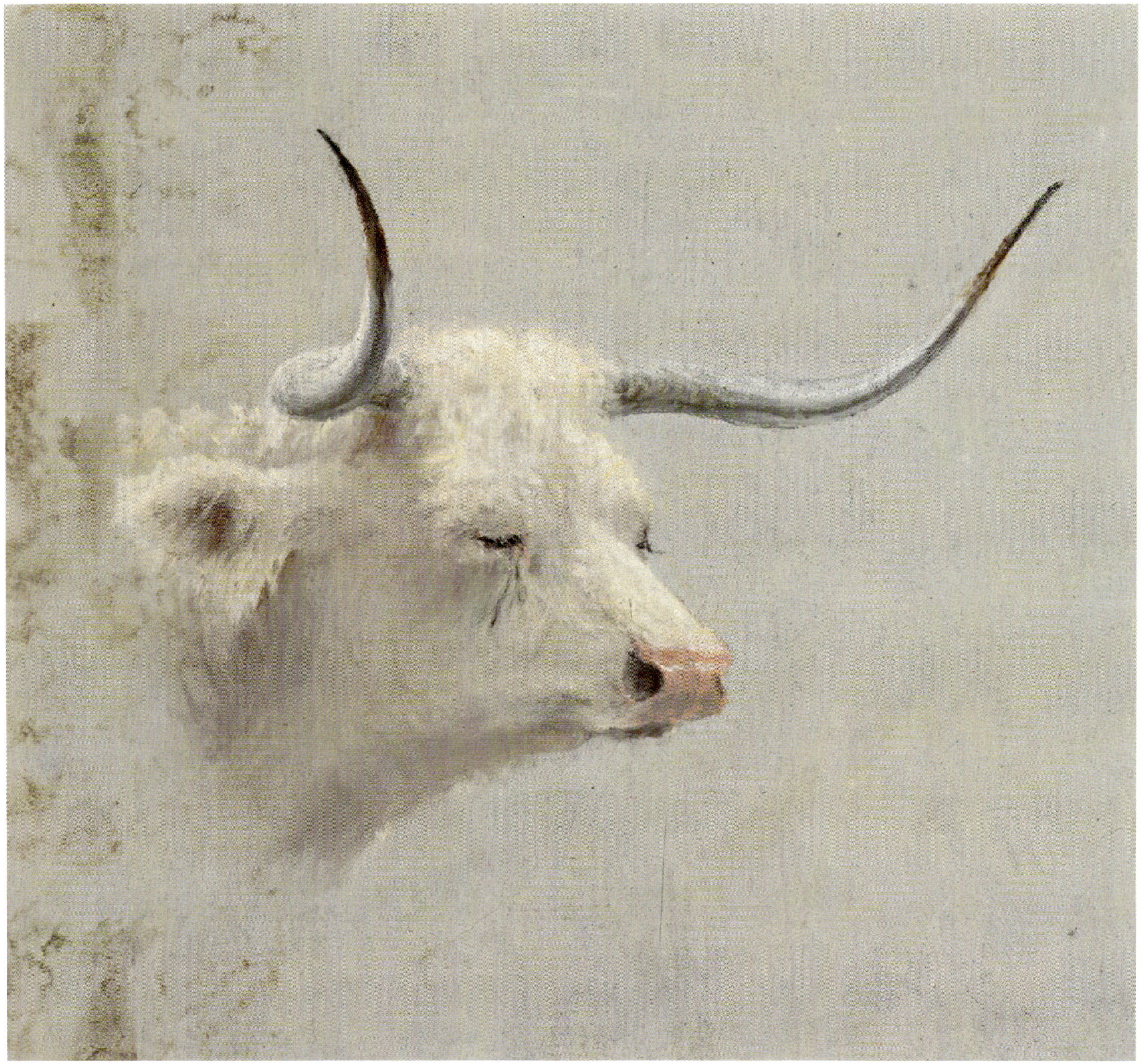

Plate 25

In the Rain

Oil

9½ × 21½

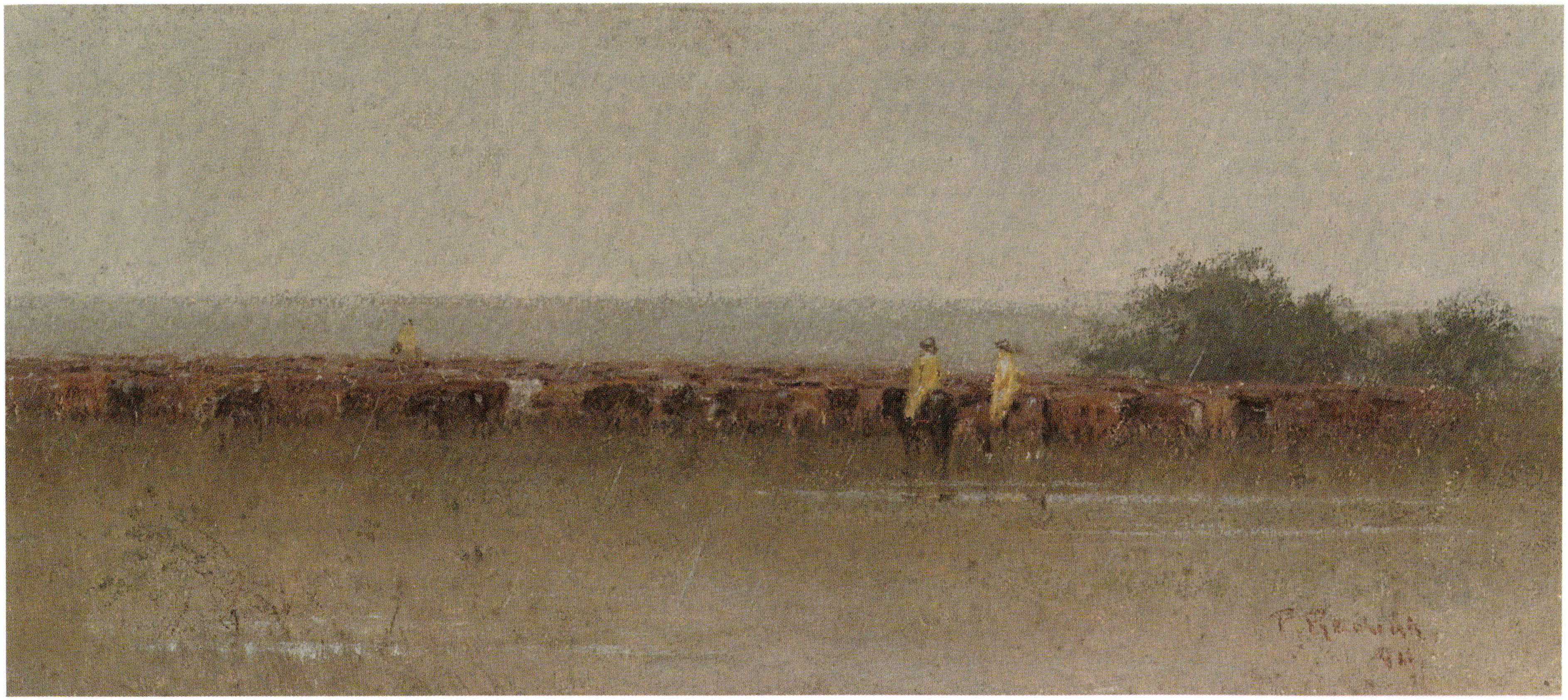

PLATE 26

Paderewski

Pastel

5 × 6

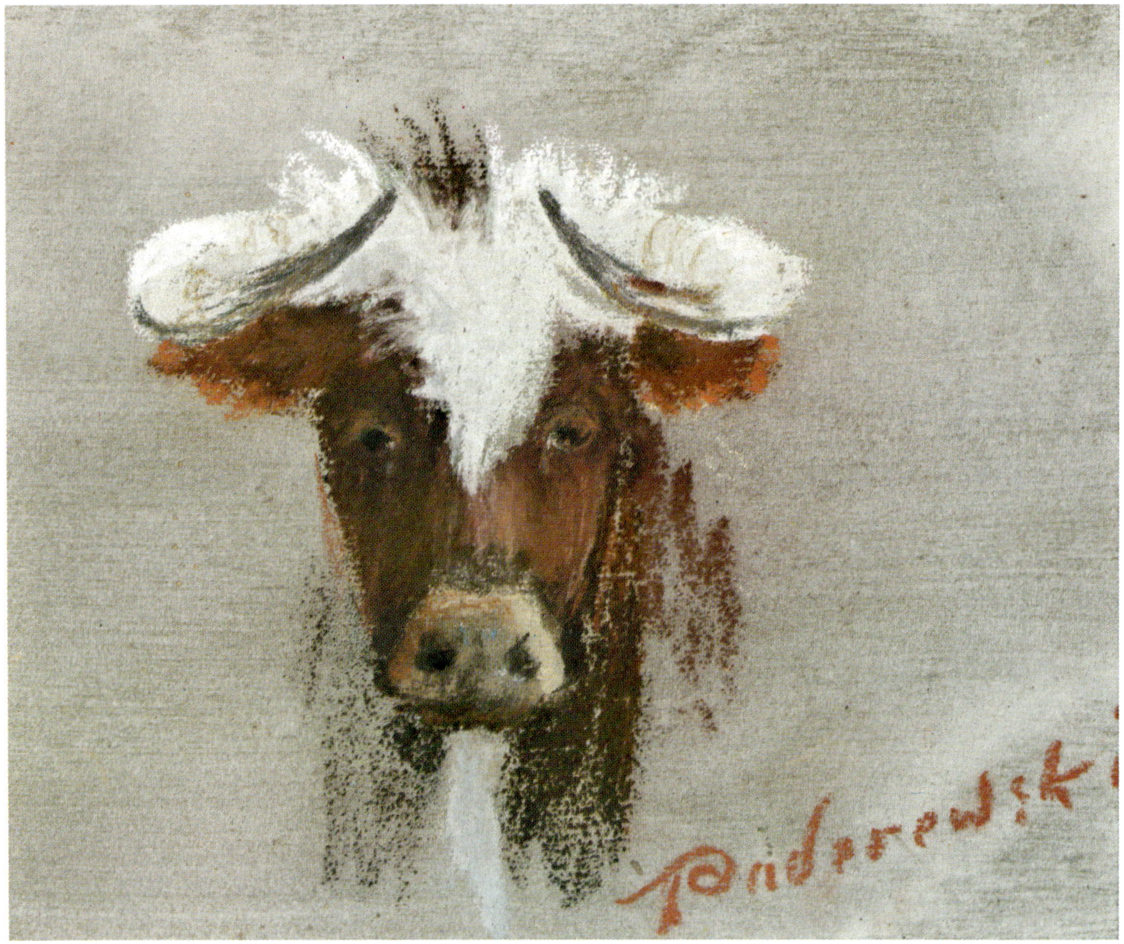

PLATE 27

Fort Worth from West

Pastel

4 × 8

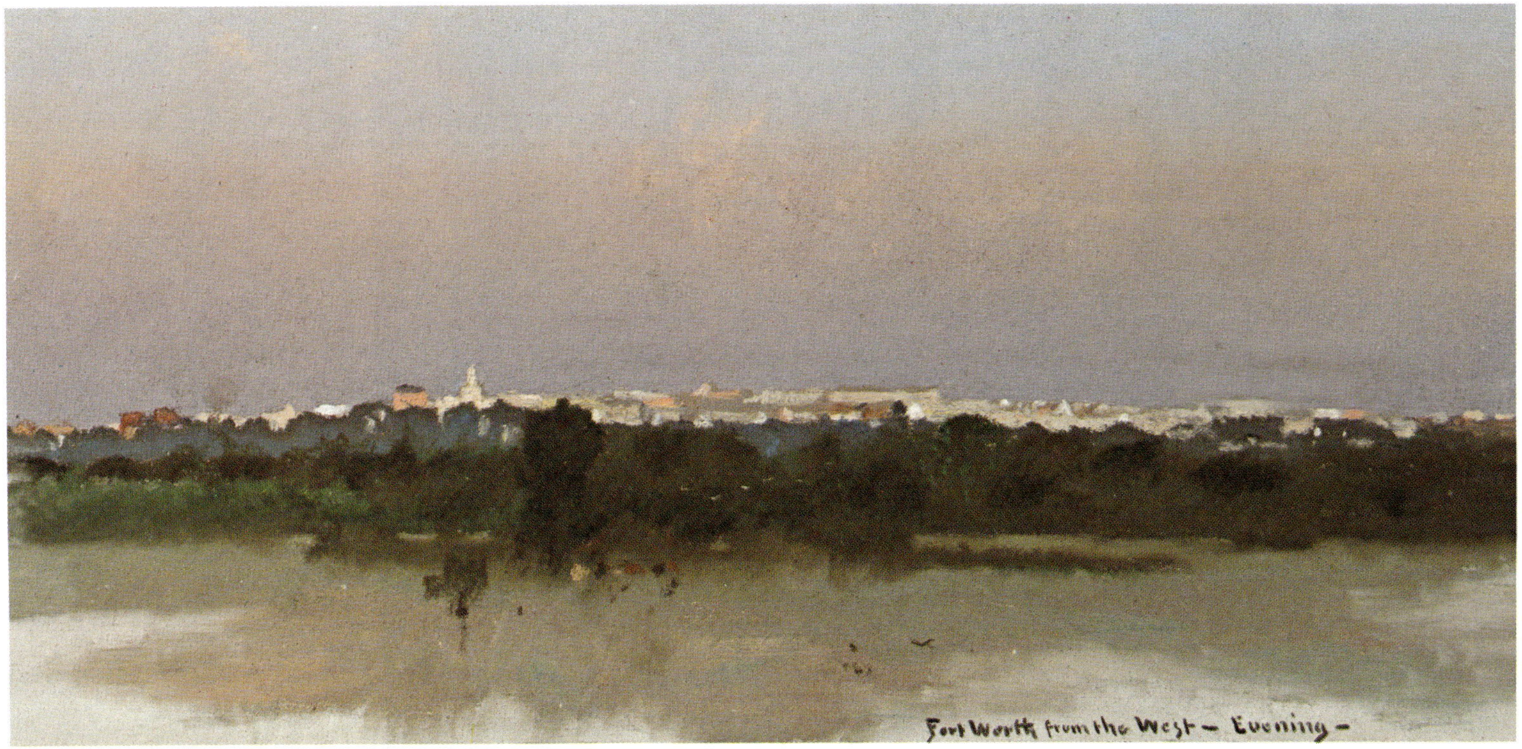
Fort Worth from the West – Evening –

Plate 28

Brushy Bottom

Pastel

16 × 21 ¼

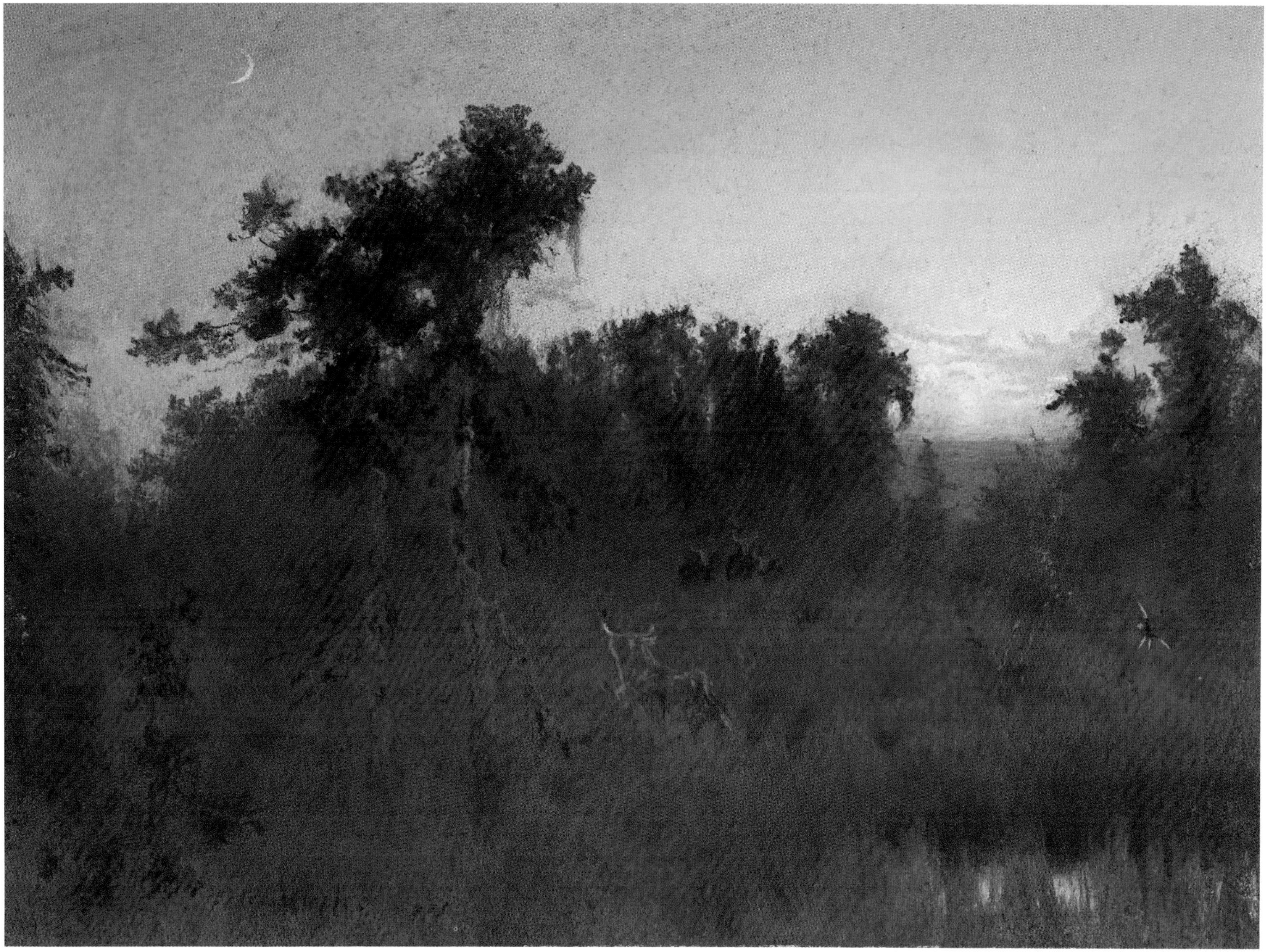

PLATE 29
Enchanted Mesa
Pastel
11½ × 19½

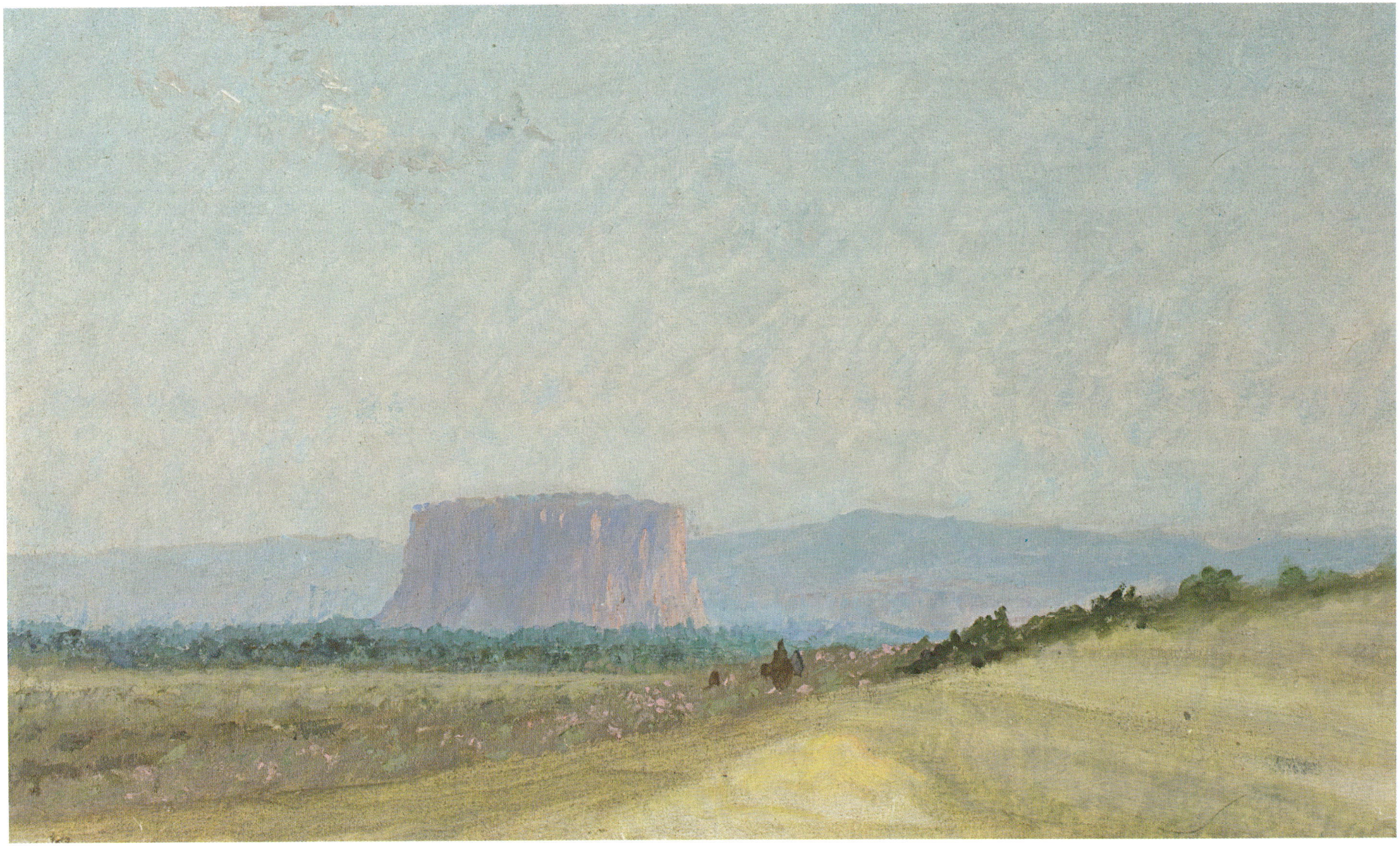

PLATE 30

The Challenge, 1936

Pastel

24 × 48

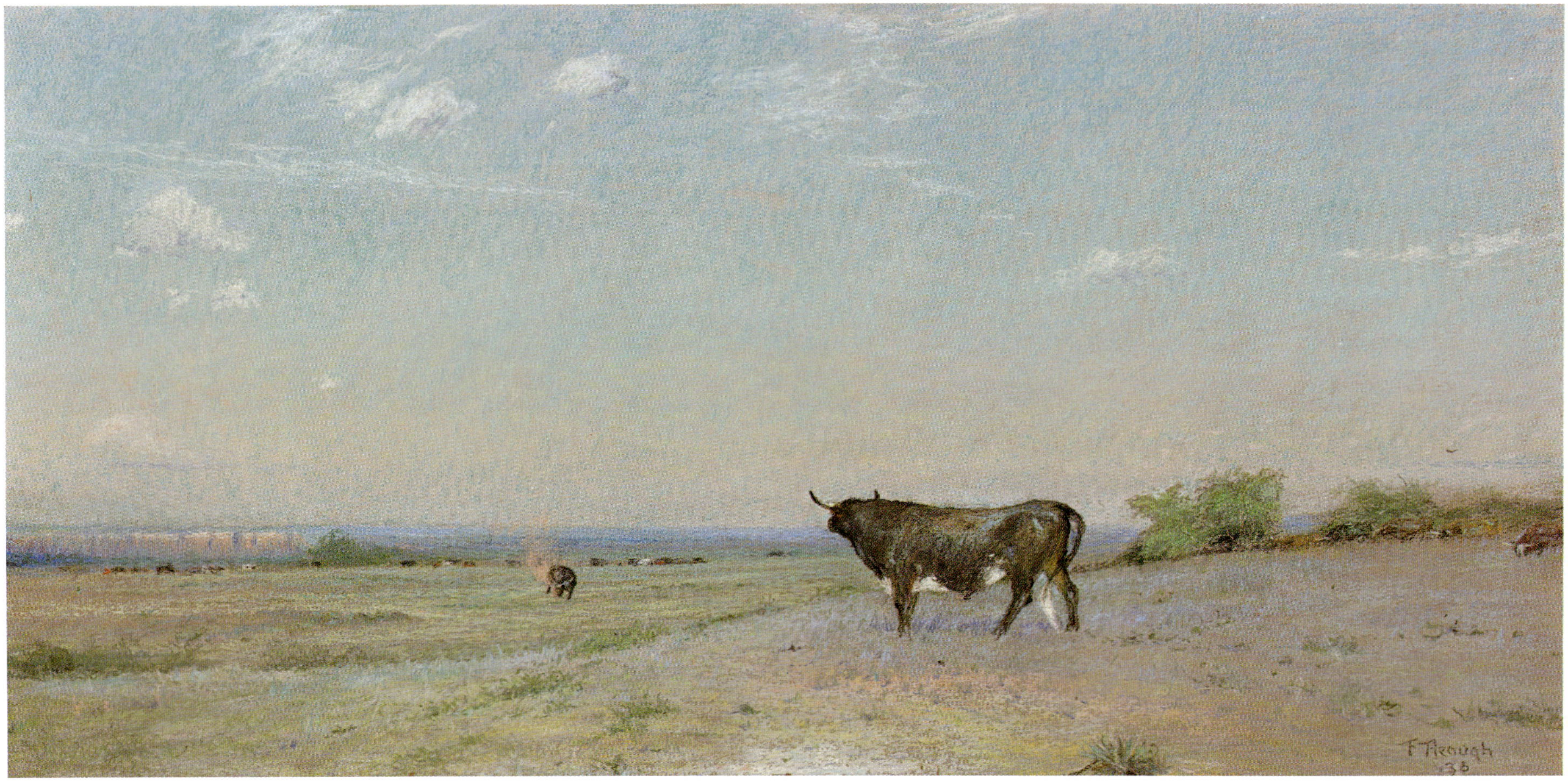
F Reaugh
36

PLATE 31

Sunset

Pastel

13 × 29

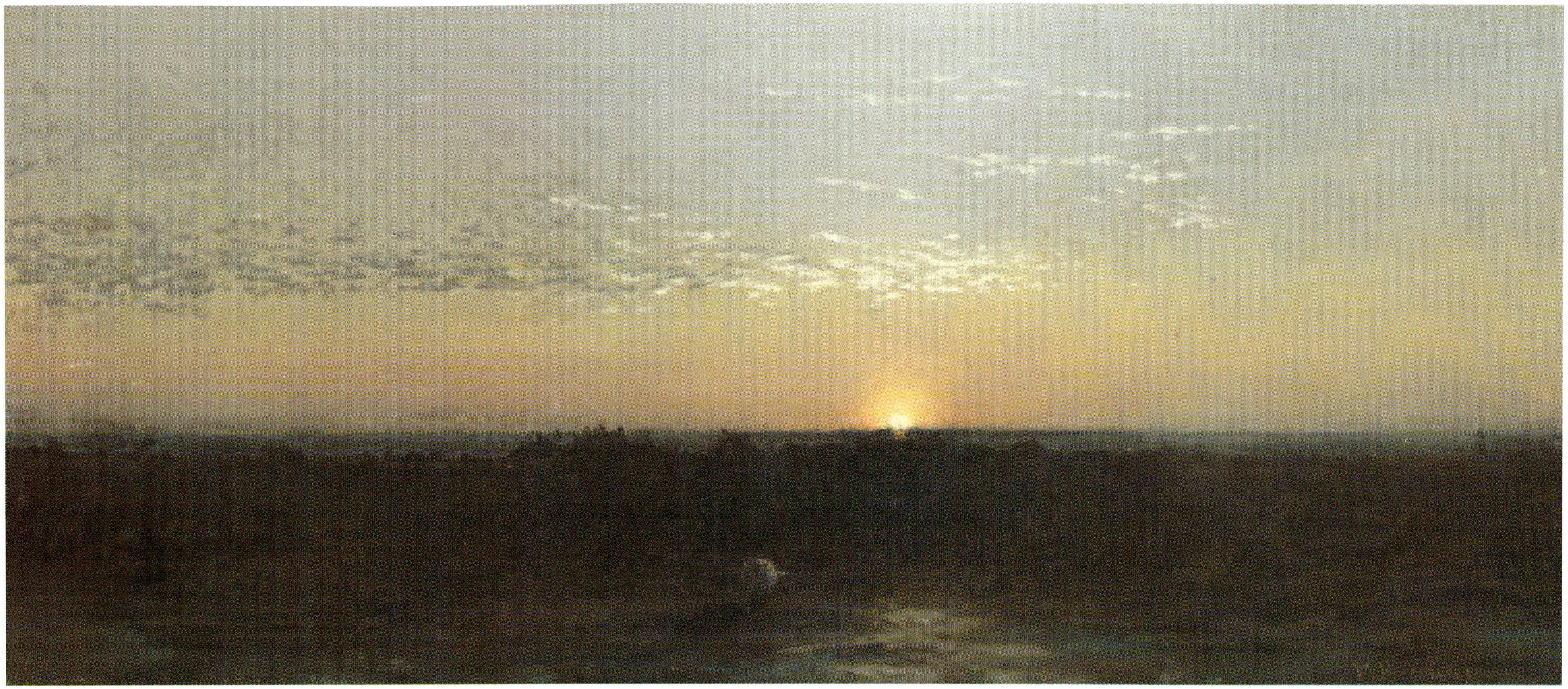

PLATE 32

Waning Moon

Pastel

14 × 24

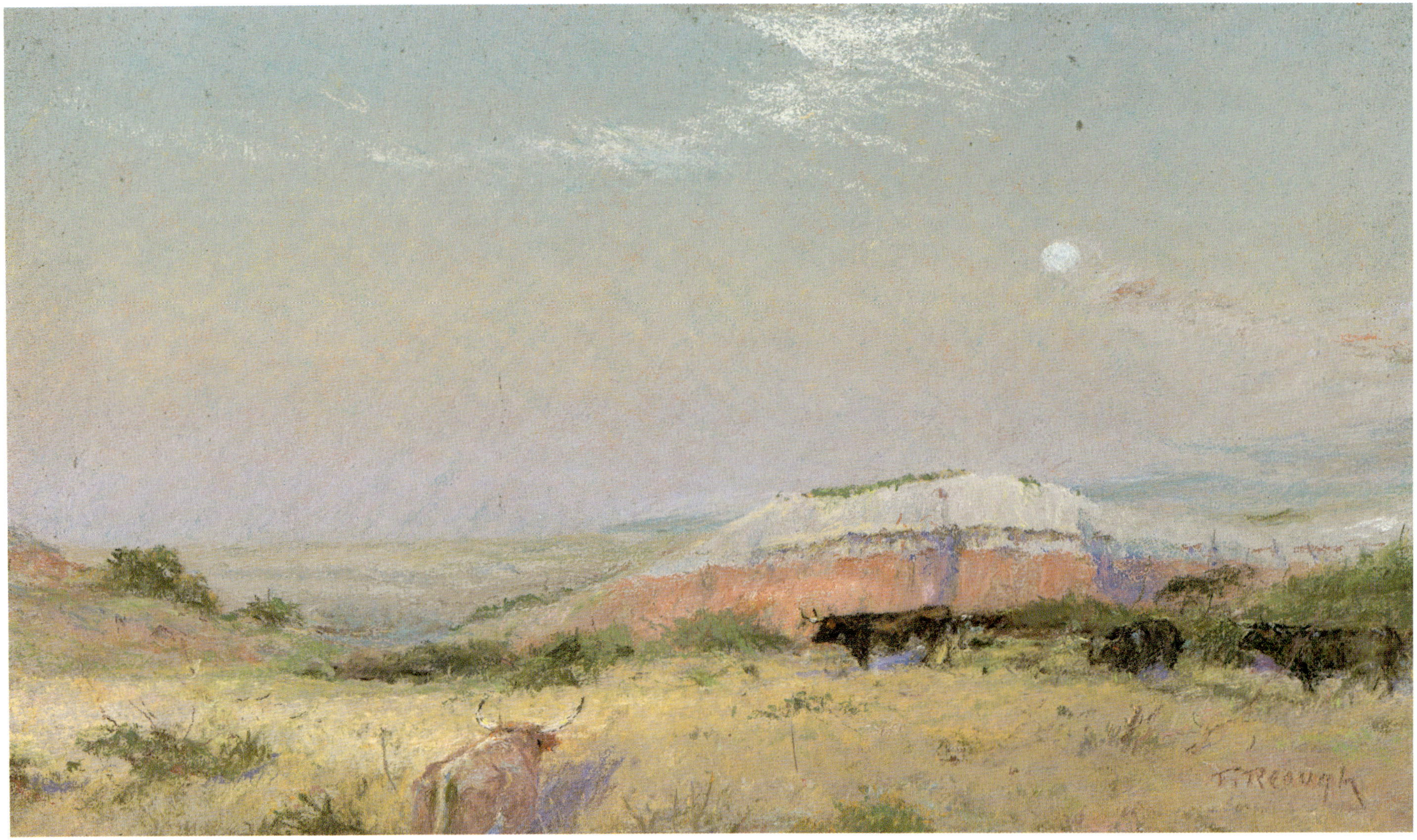

PLATE 33
Twilight—Rest
Pastel
15 ½ × 31 ½

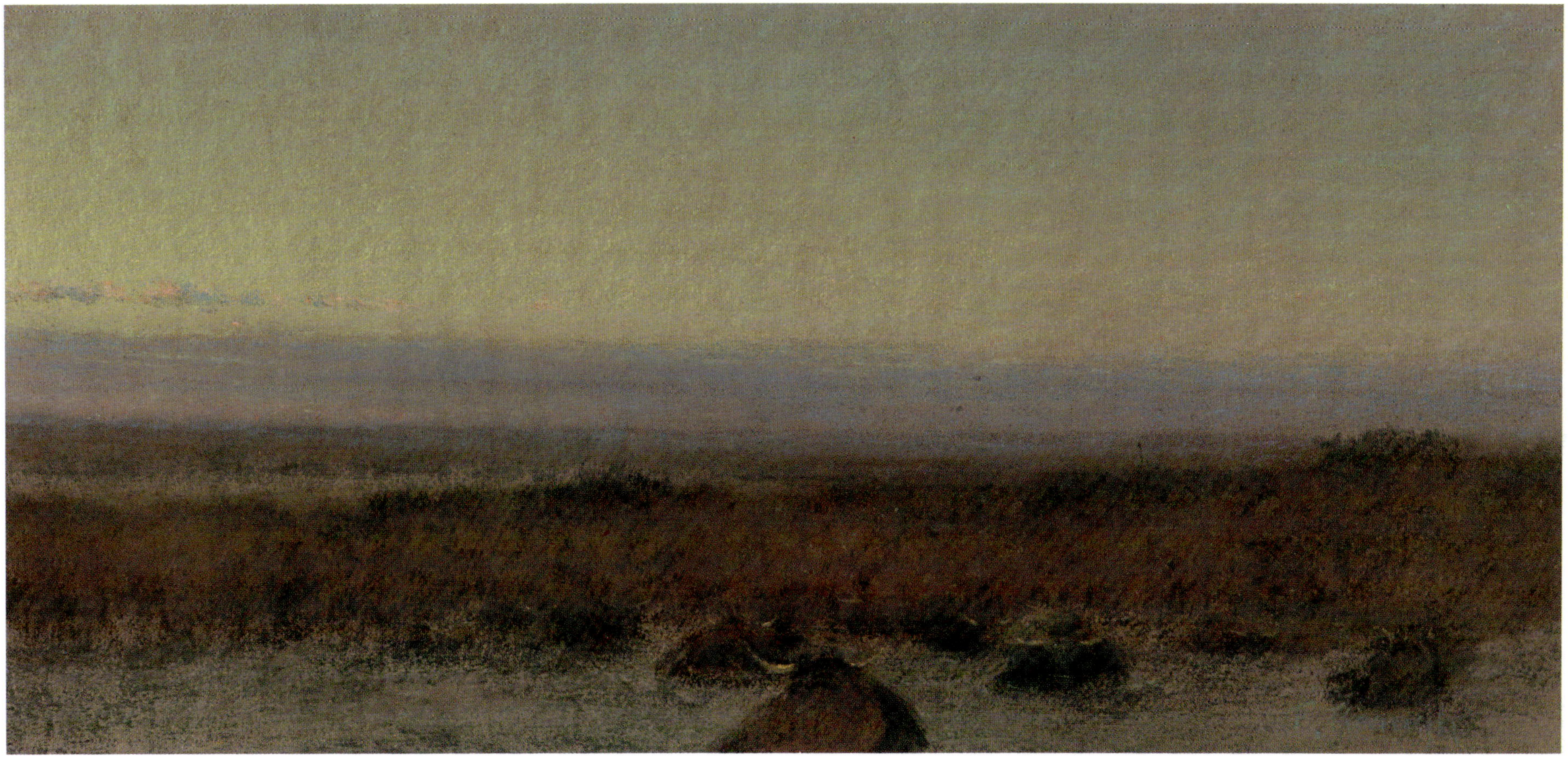

Plate 34
Barnyard in Winter
Pastel
8 × 14

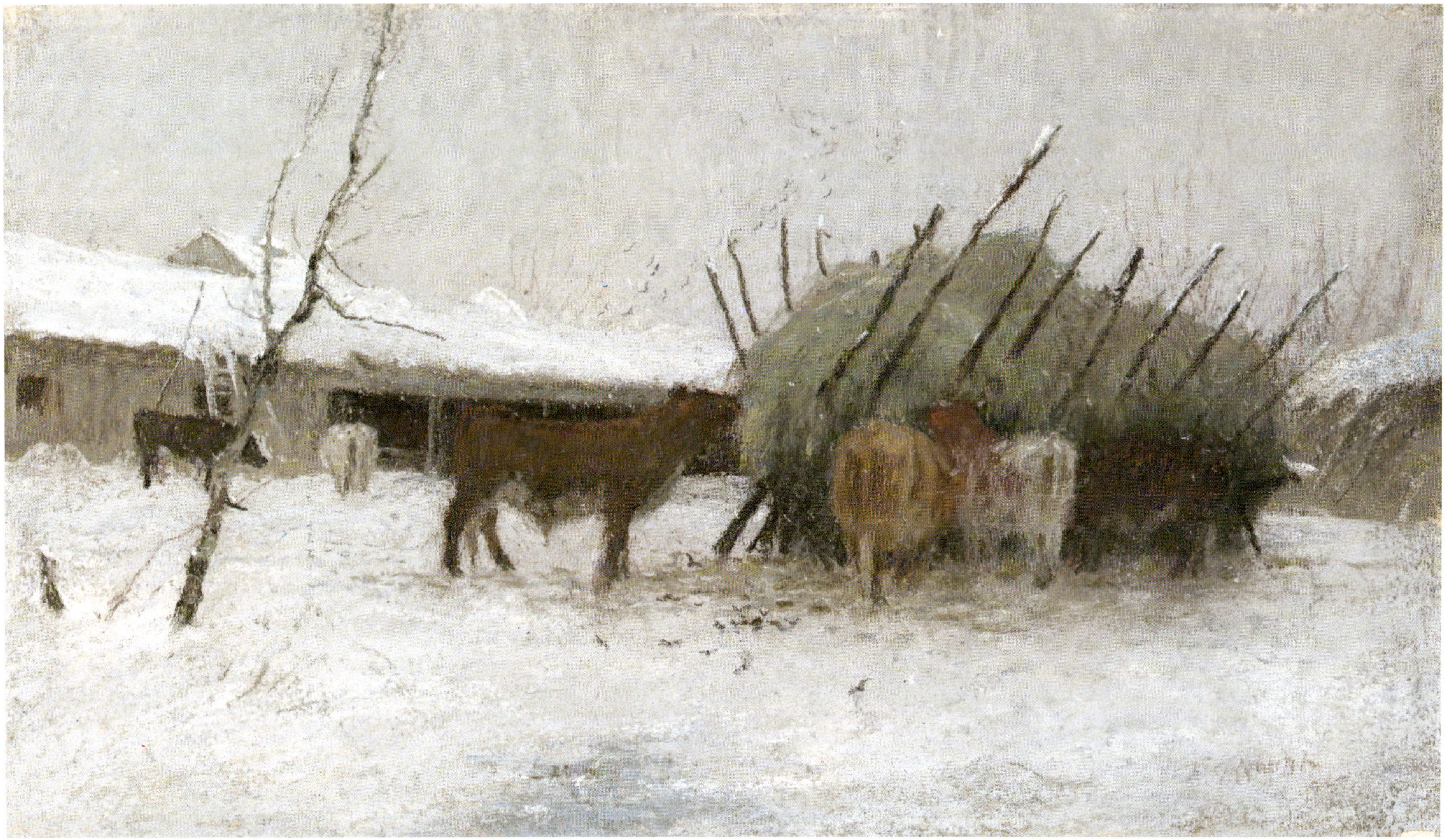

PLATE 35

Driving the Herd

(Twenty-four Hours with the Herd—I)

Pastel

24 × 48

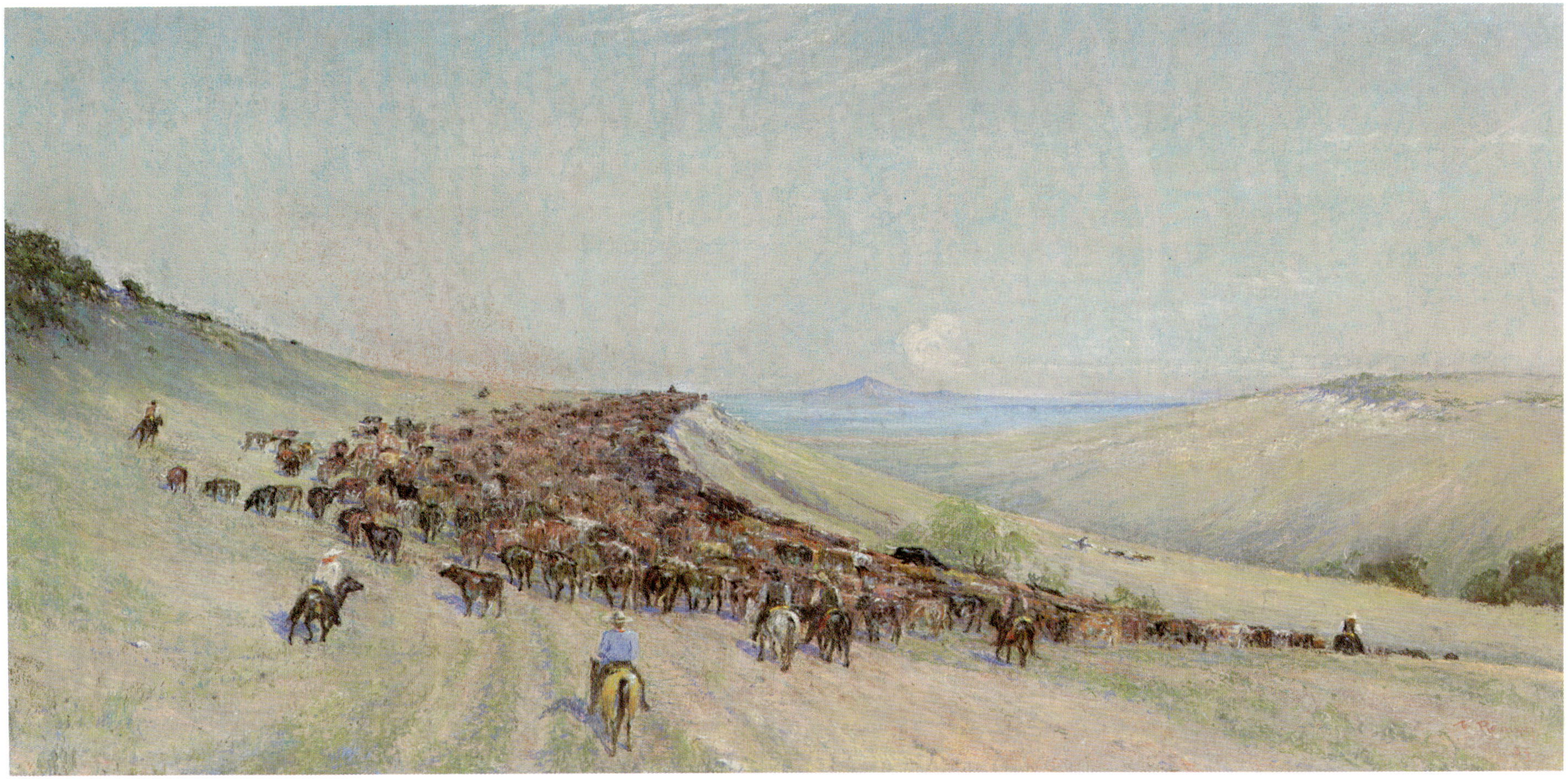

PLATE 36

Watering the Herd, 1932

(Twenty-four Hours with the Herd—II)

Pastel

24 × 48

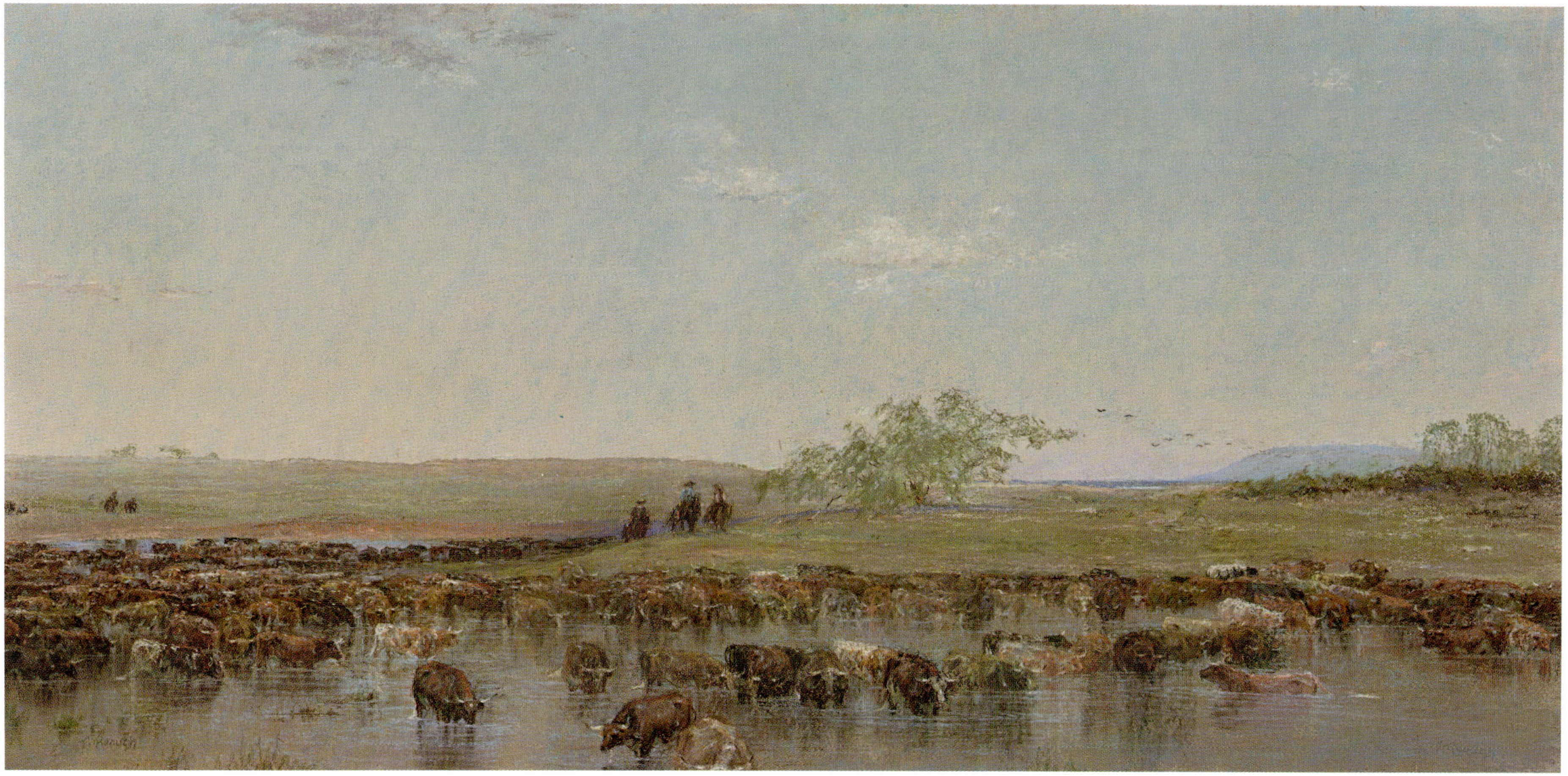

PLATE 37

Bedding the Herd

(Twenty-four Hours with the Herd—III)

Pastel

24 × 48

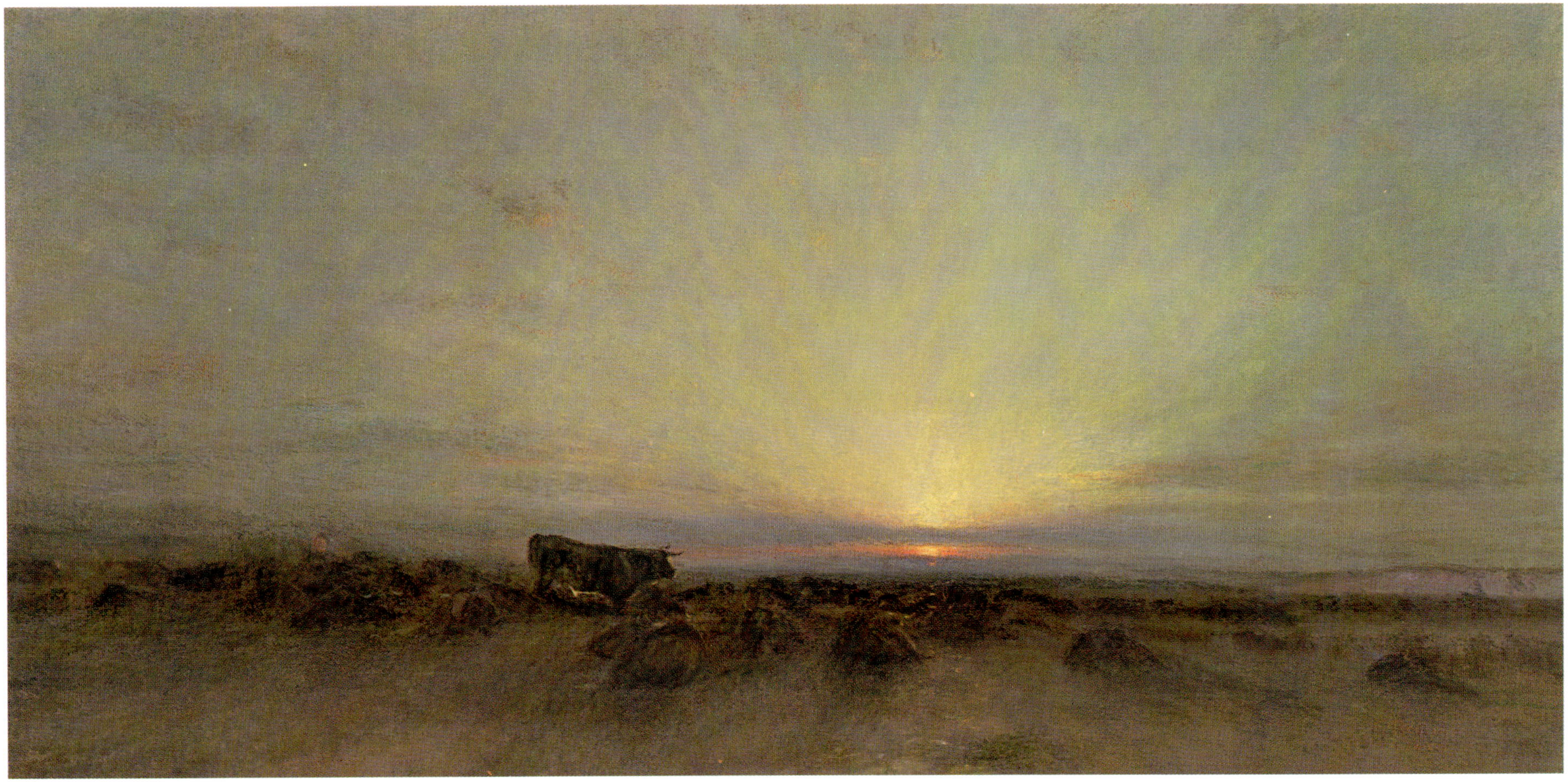

PLATE 38

Guarding the Herd

(Twenty-four Hours with the Herd—IV)

Pastel

24 × 48

PLATE 39

Stampede in the Canyon

(Twenty-four Hours with the Herd—V)

Pastel

23 ½ × 47 ½

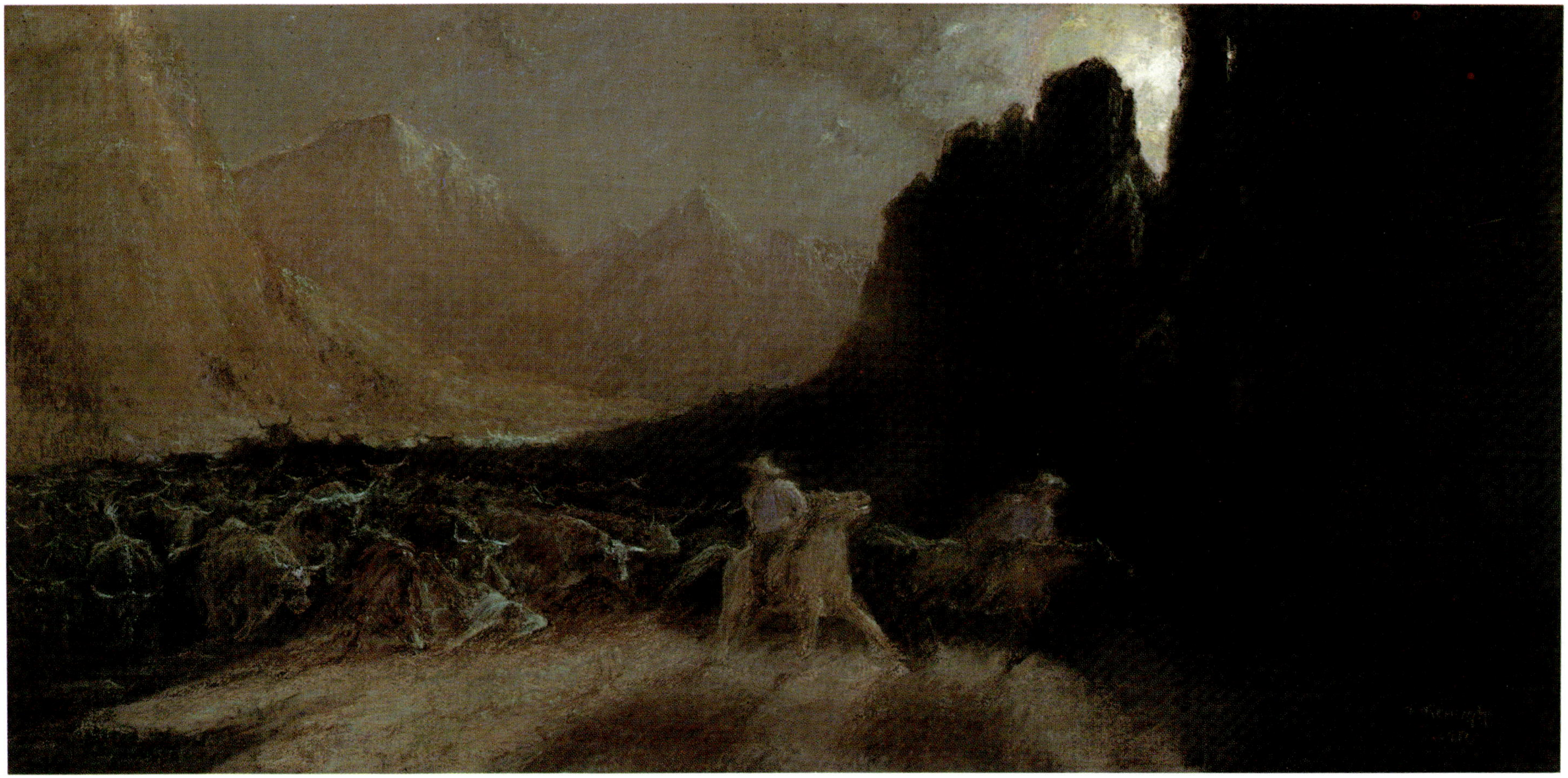

PLATE 40

Milling Cattle

(Twenty-four Hours with the Herd—VI)

Pastel

23 ½ × 47 ¼

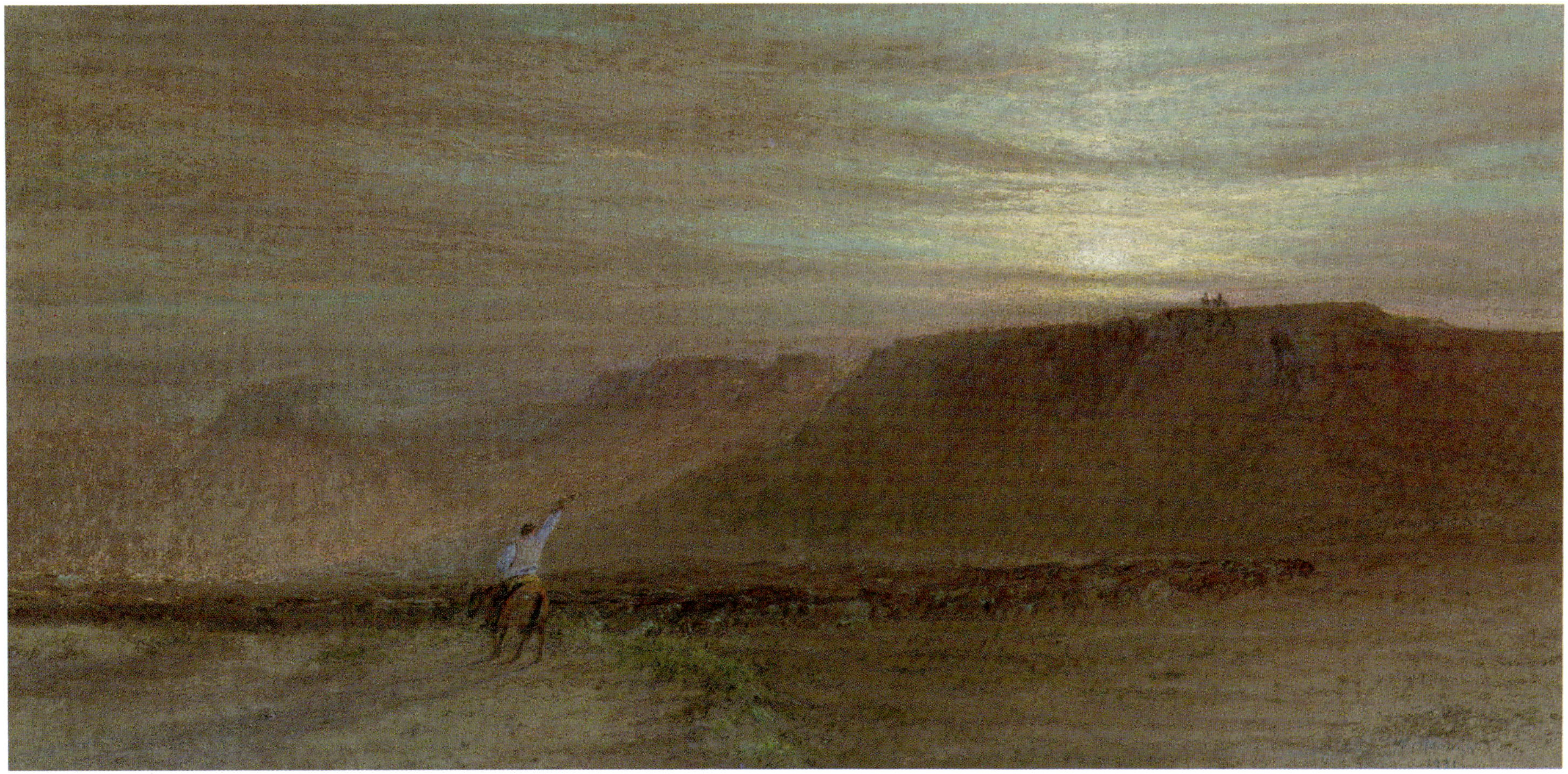

PLATE 41

The Herd Moves On

(Twenty-four Hours with the Herd—VII)

Pastel

23 × 48

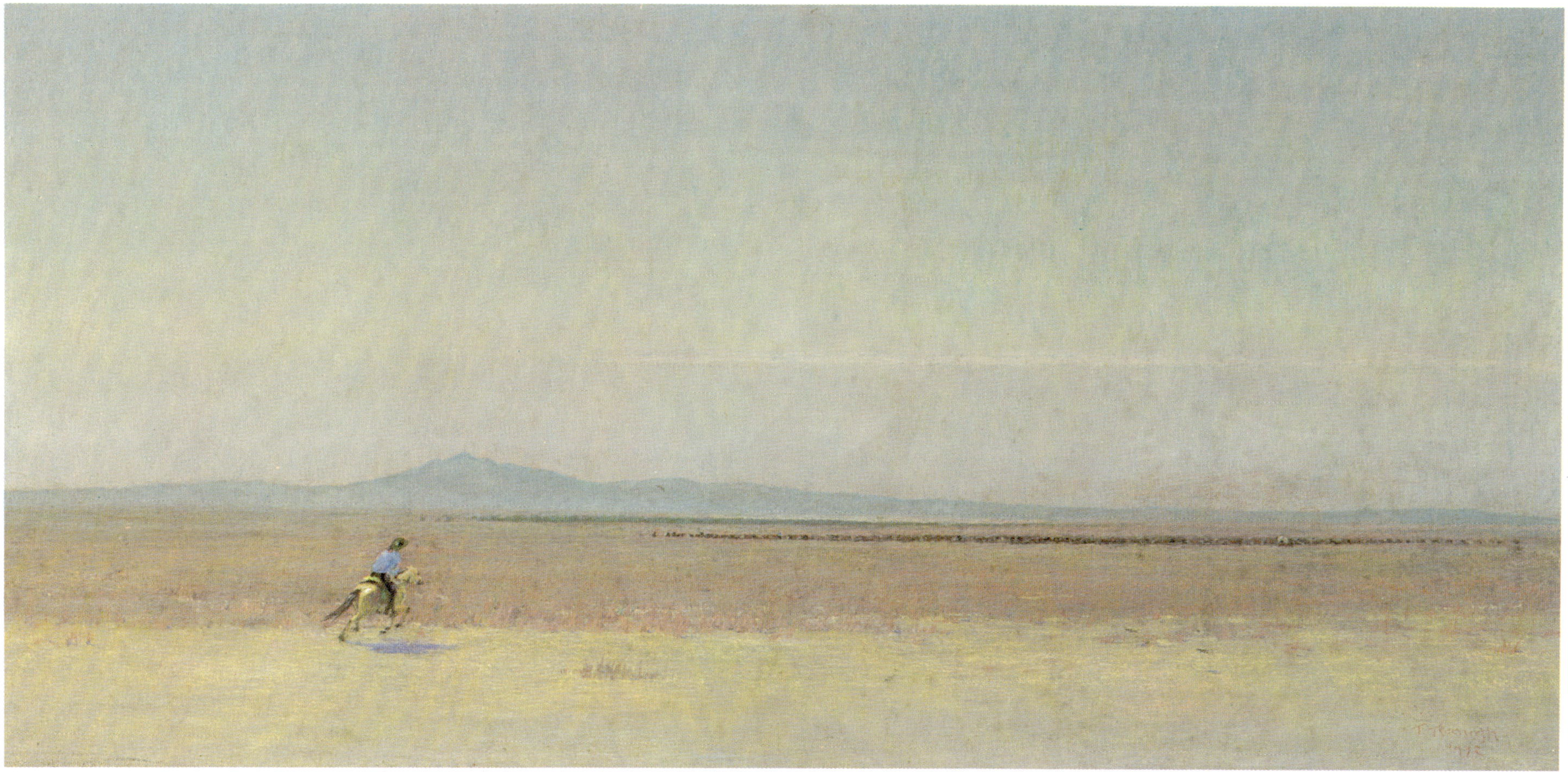

PLATE 42

Prophet's Ford

Pastel

16¼ × 31½

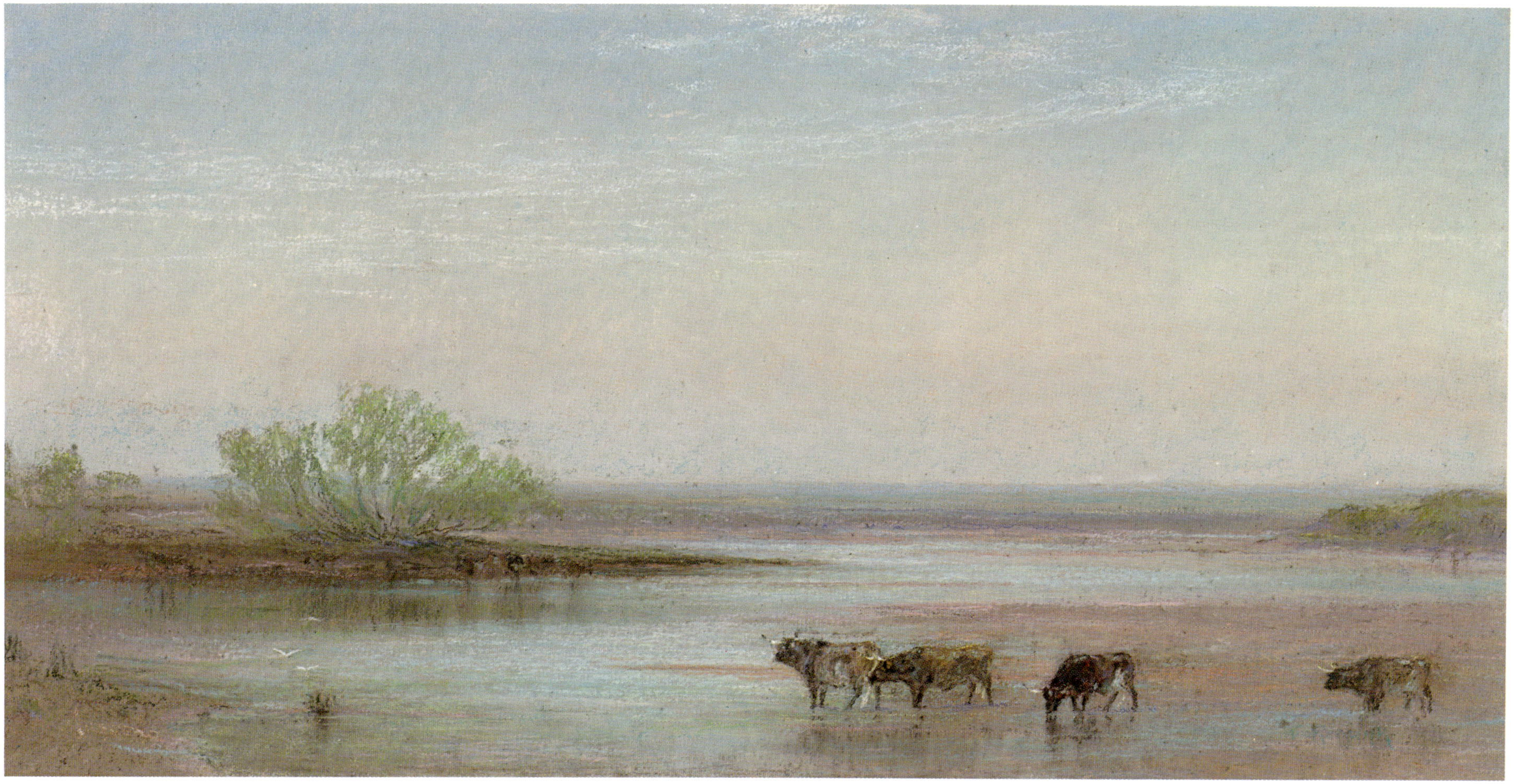

PLATE 43
Passing Cattle
Pastel
23 ½ × 47 ¼

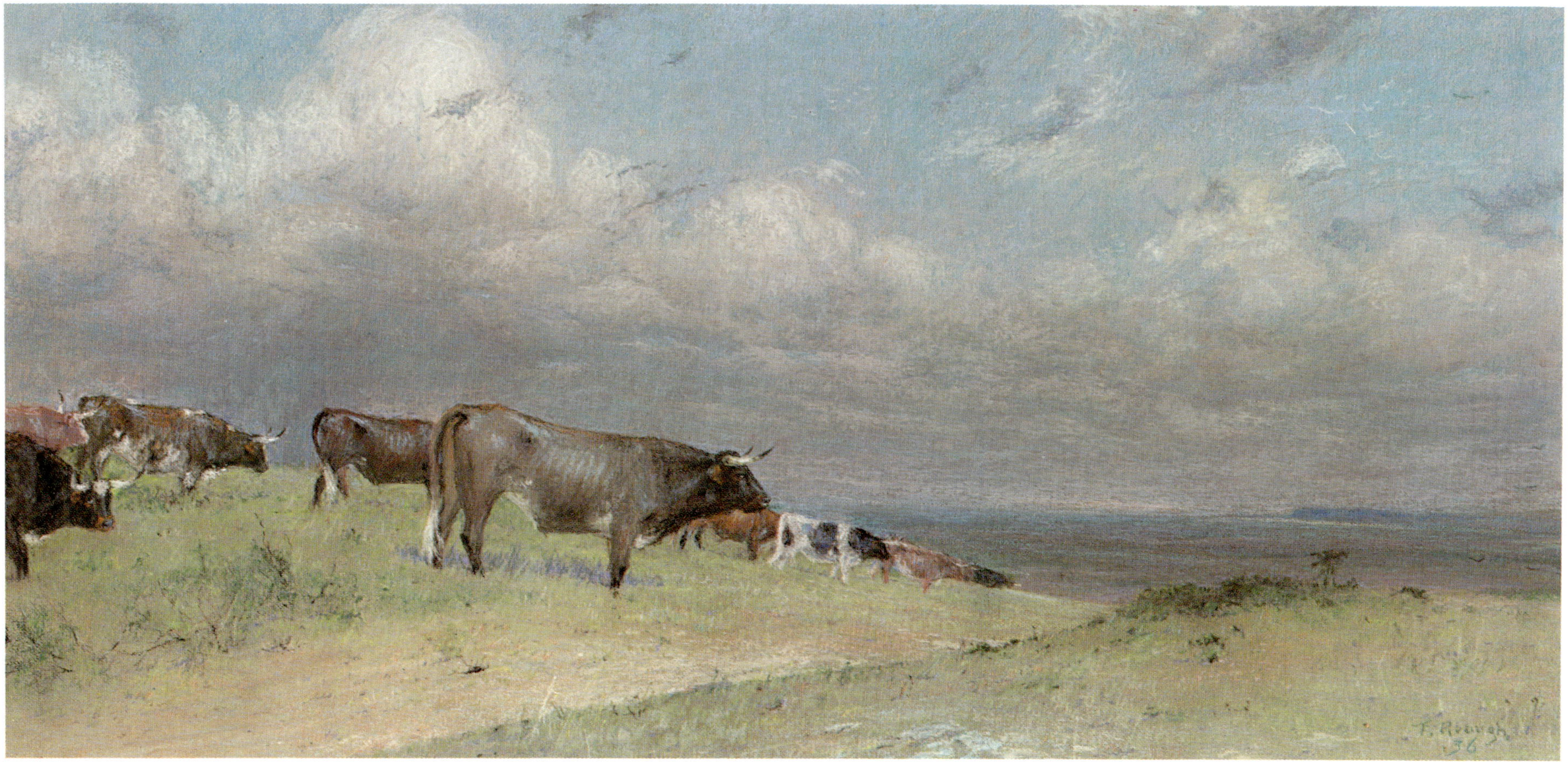

PLATE 44

Palo Pinto Pasture, 1937

Pastel

13 × 24

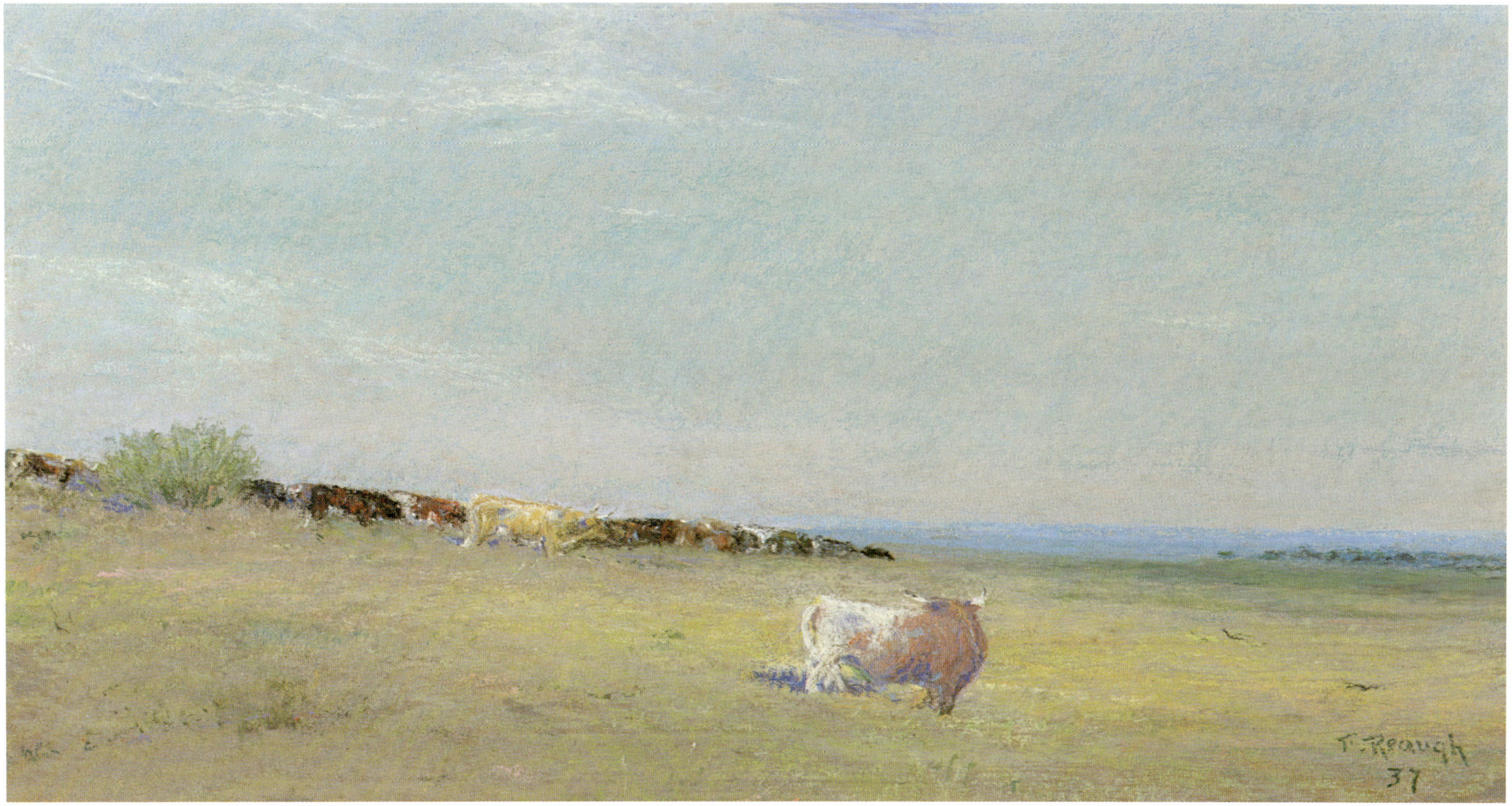
F. Reaugh
37

PLATE 45

Sketch of Reclining Bull

Pastel

6¼ × 10½

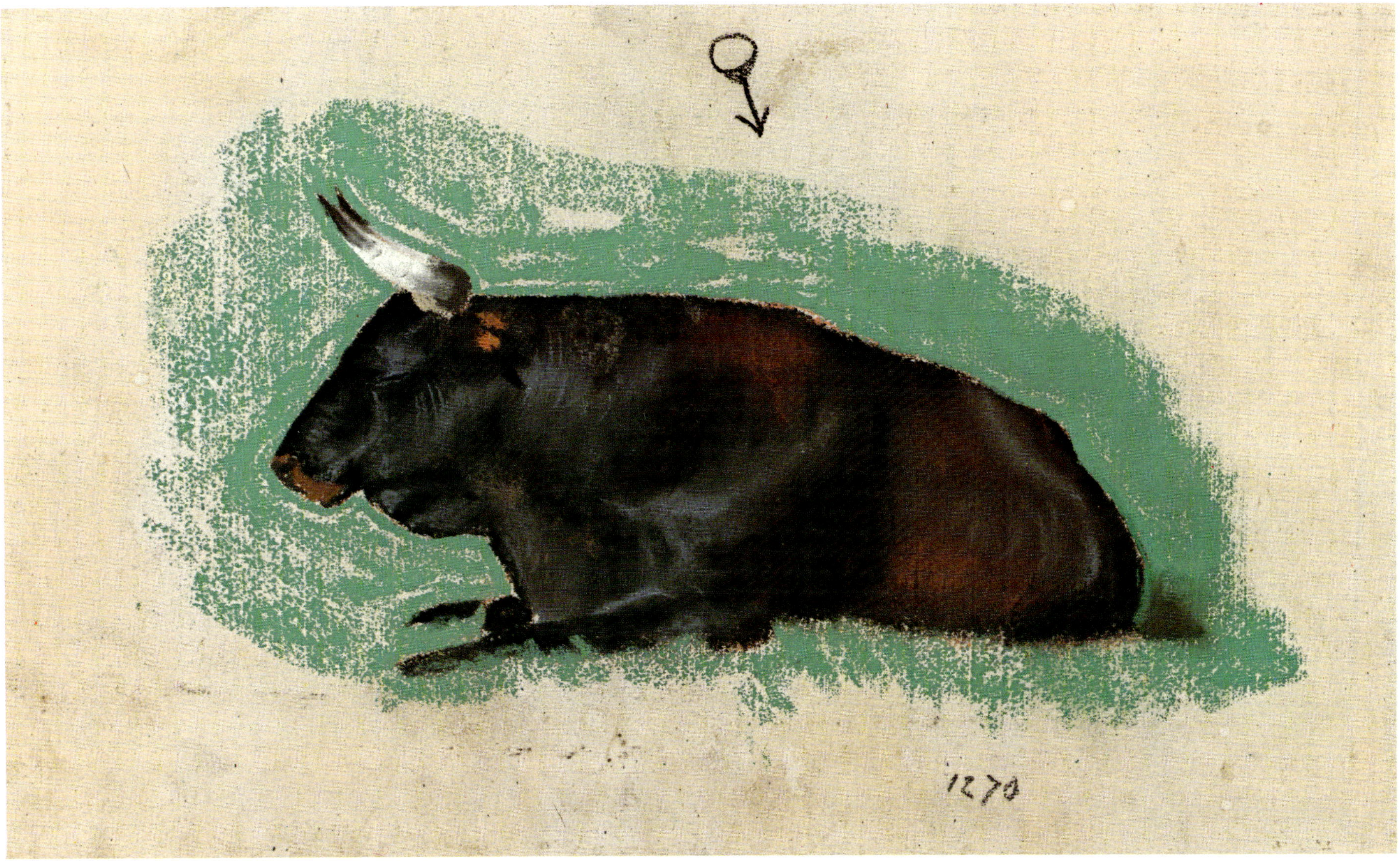
1270

PLATE 46
Summer Forenoon
Pastel
8 × 12 ¼

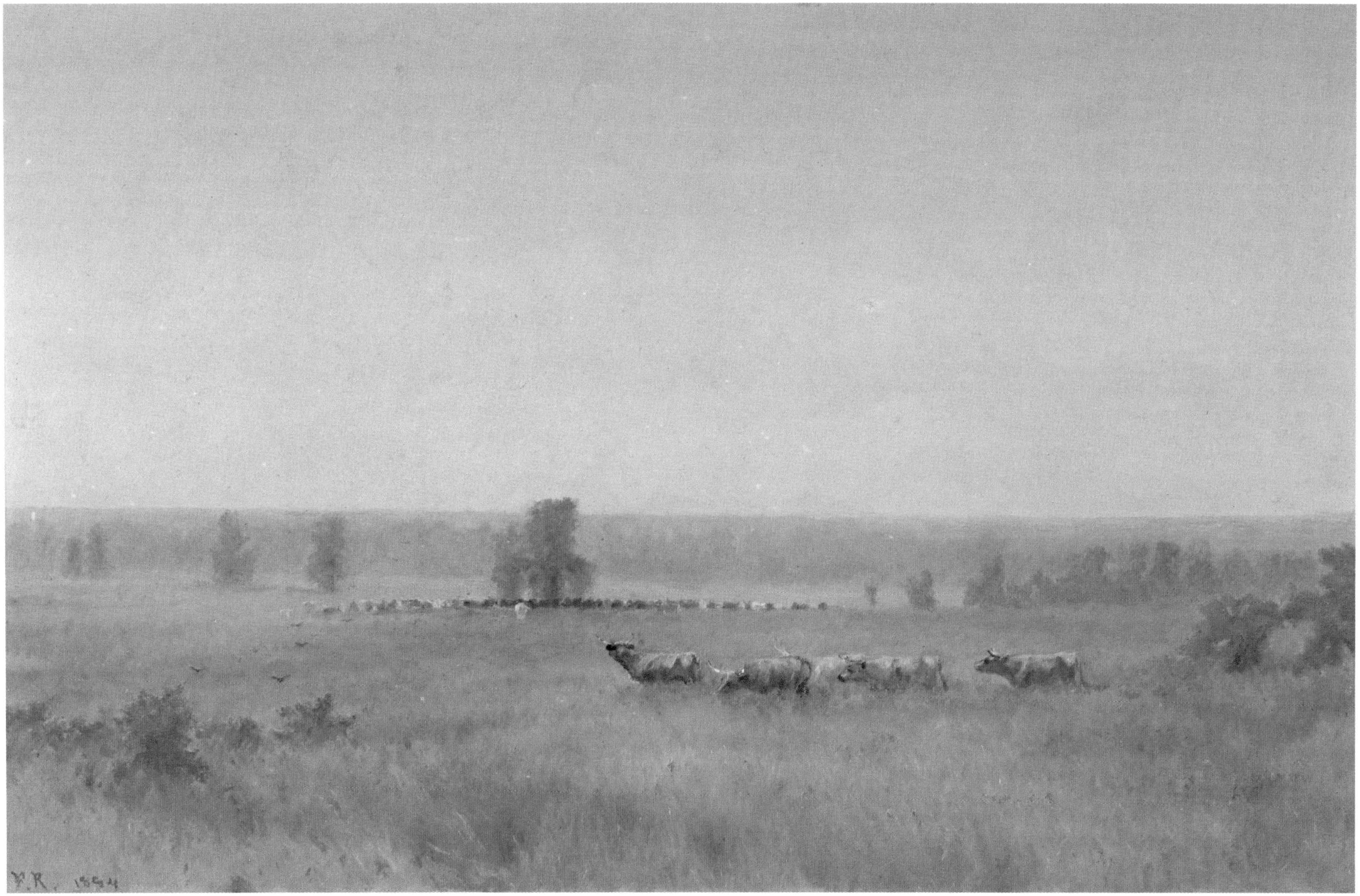

PLATE 47

A Stampede

Pastel

16 × 32

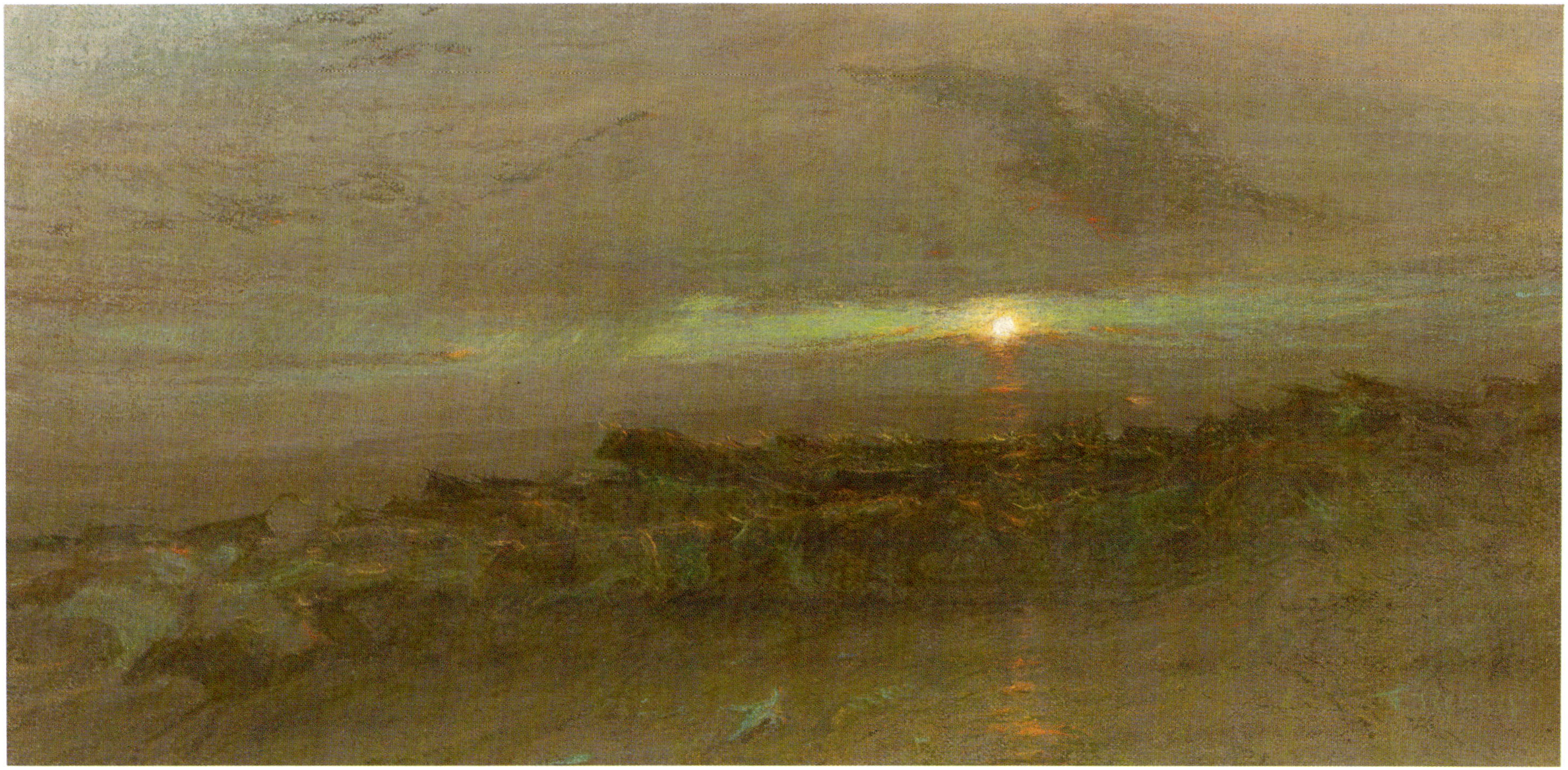

PLATE 48

Spring Foliage and Cows

Pastel

9 × 16

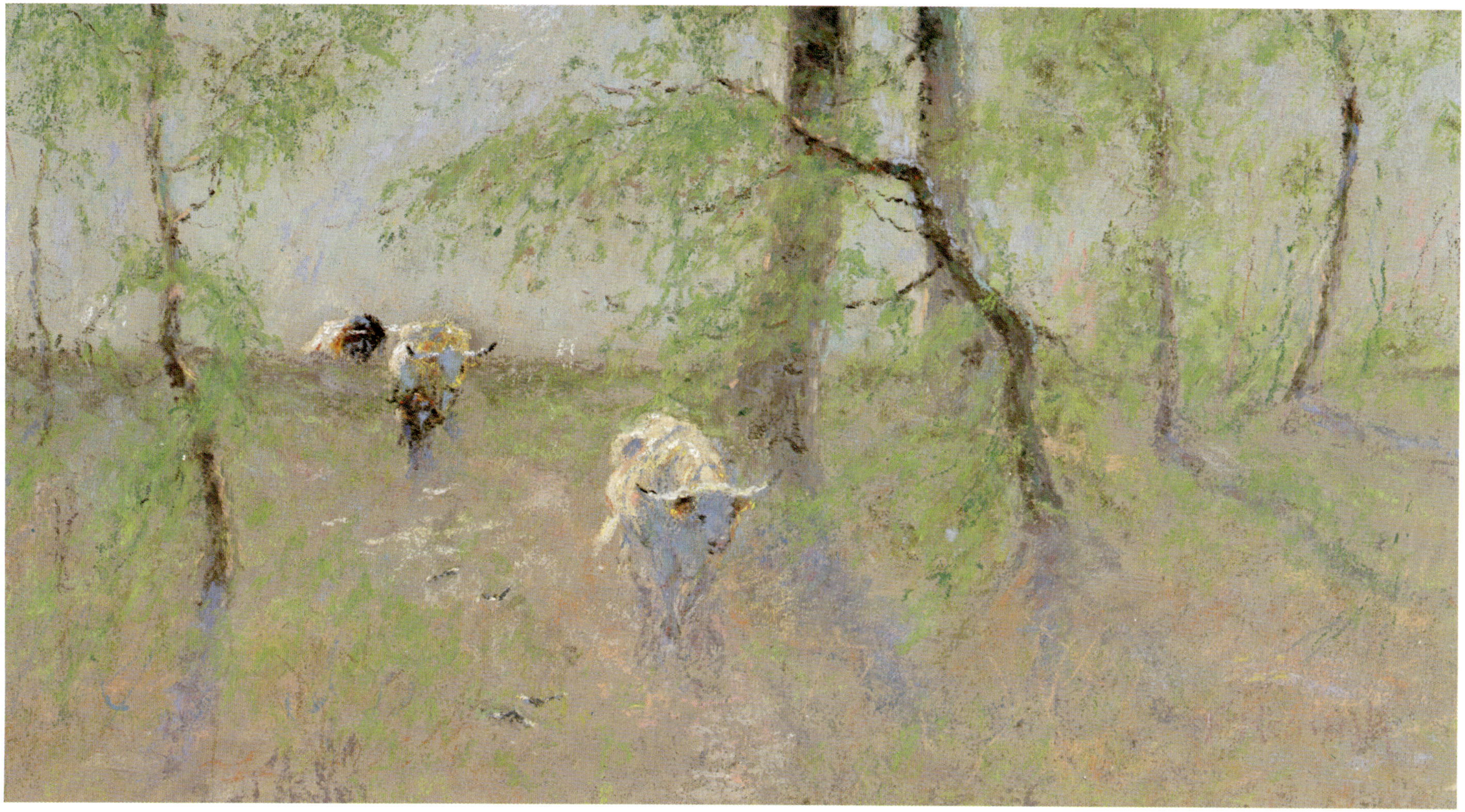

PLATE 49

Live Oak Pool

Pastel

3 × 6½

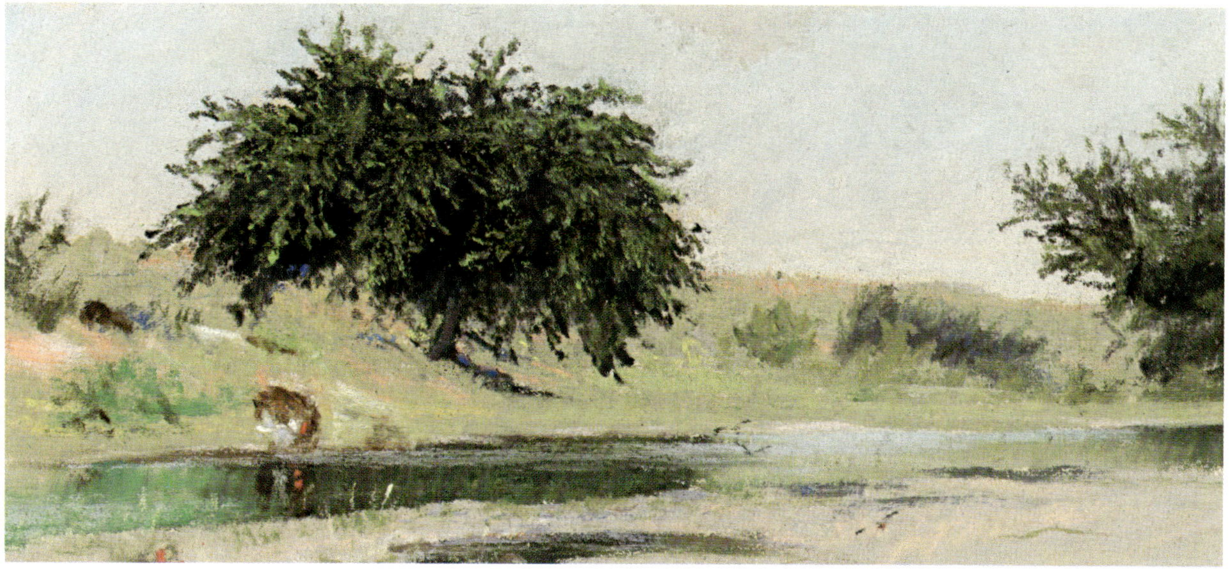

PLATE 50

White Steer and Nine Others

Pastel

2 ½ × 6

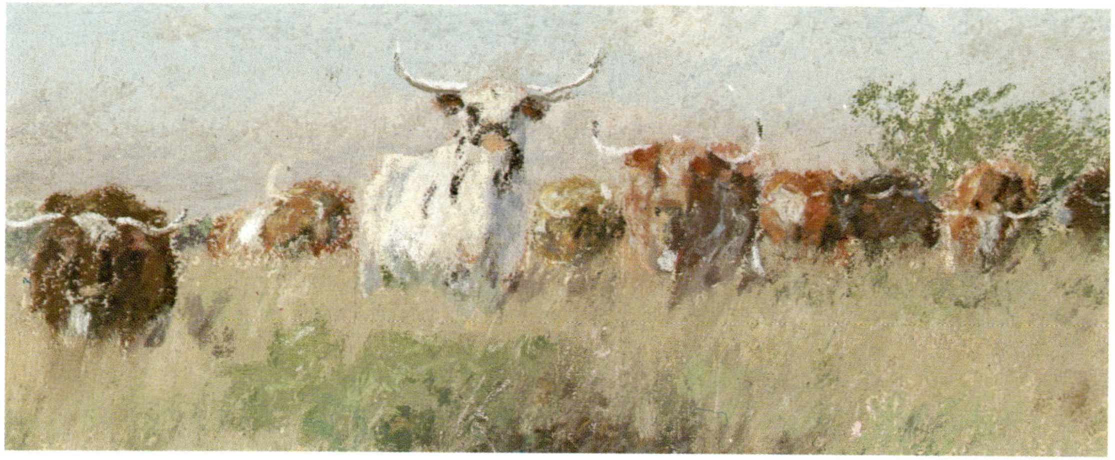

PLATE 51

San Mateo Mountains

Pastel

11 × 20

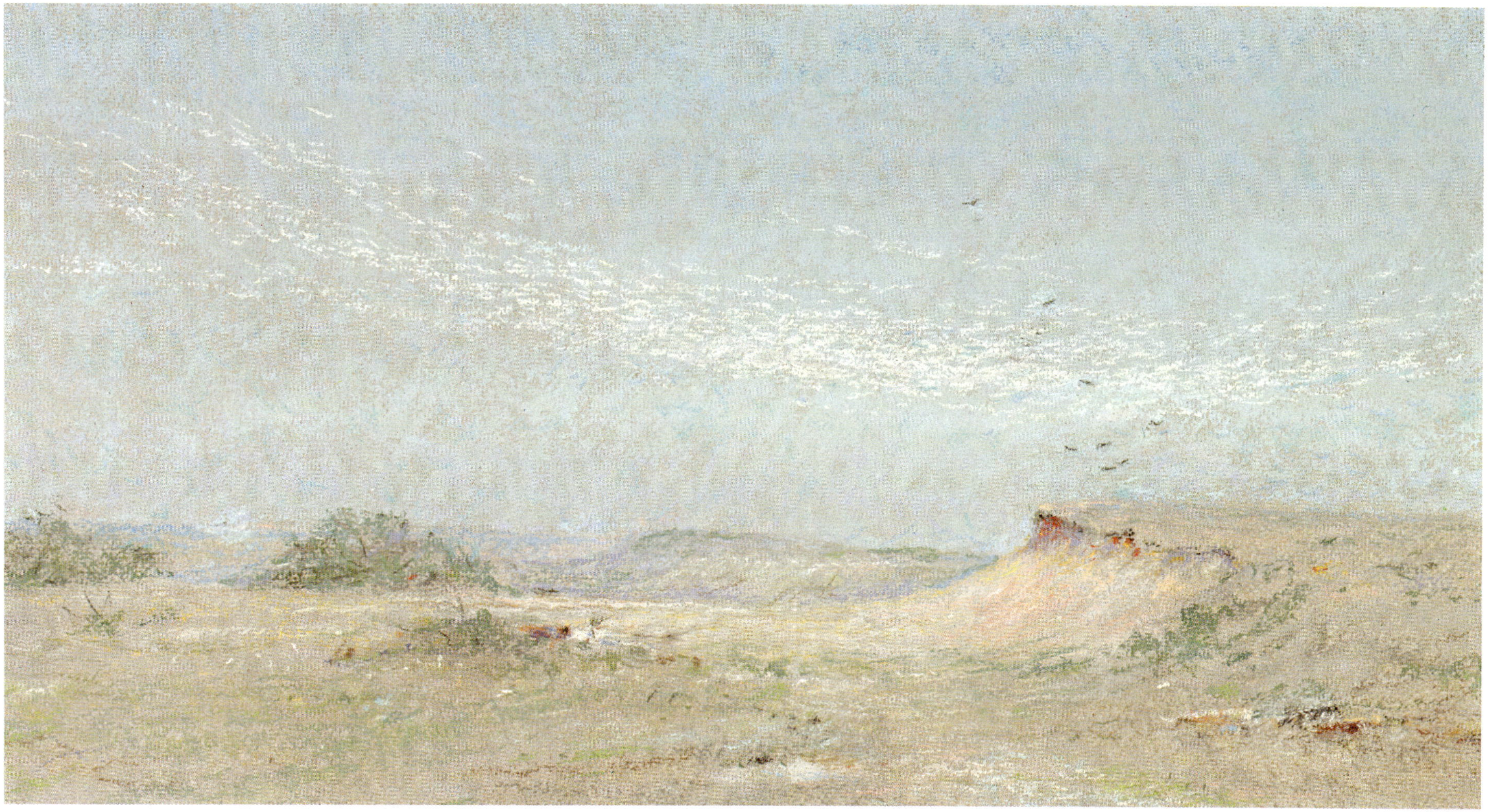

PLATE 52

Mountain Peak

Pastel

3 × 6½

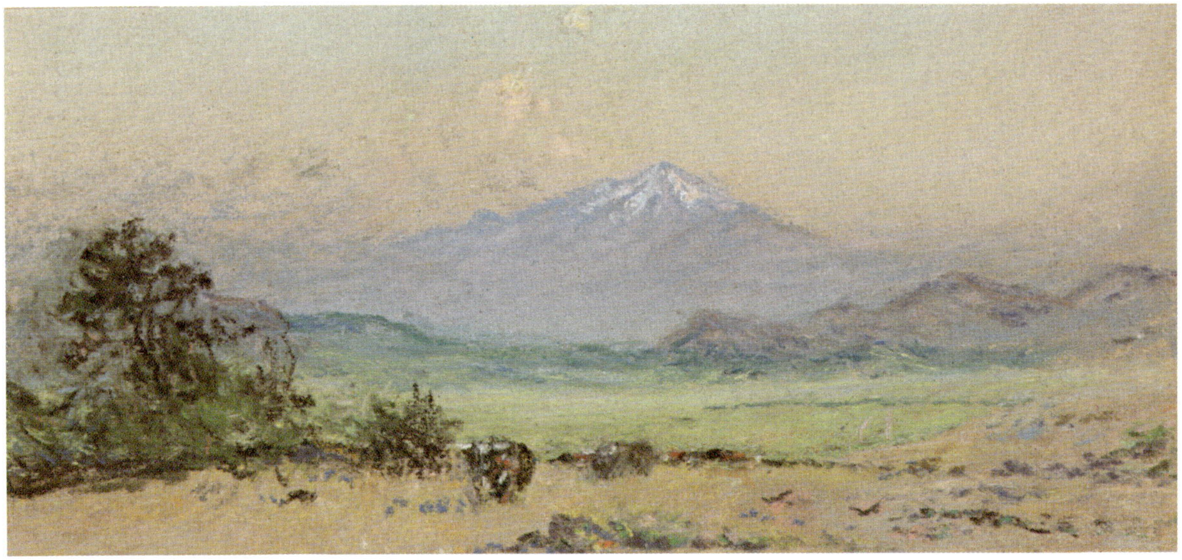

PLATE 53

Cattle Coming over Hill

Pastel

3 ½ × 7

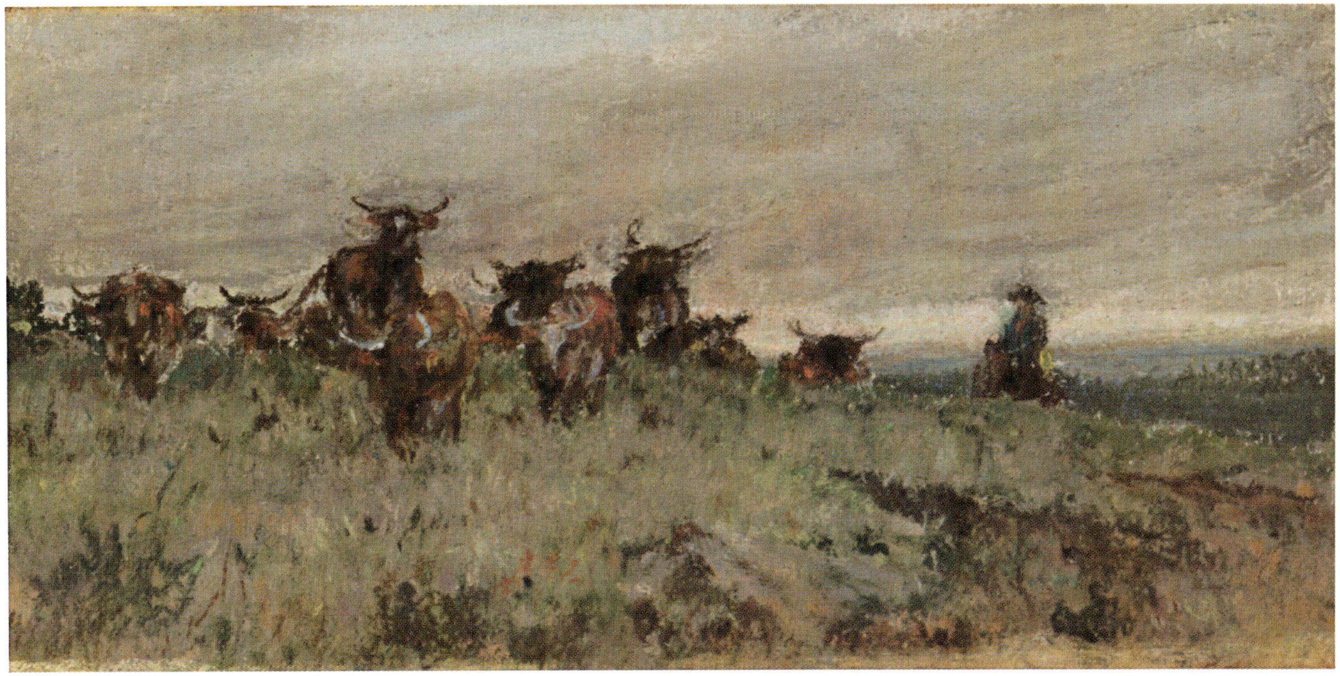

PLATE 54
Reflected Skirts
Pastel
3 ½ × 7

PLATE 55
Heel Fly Time
Pastel
3 × 6

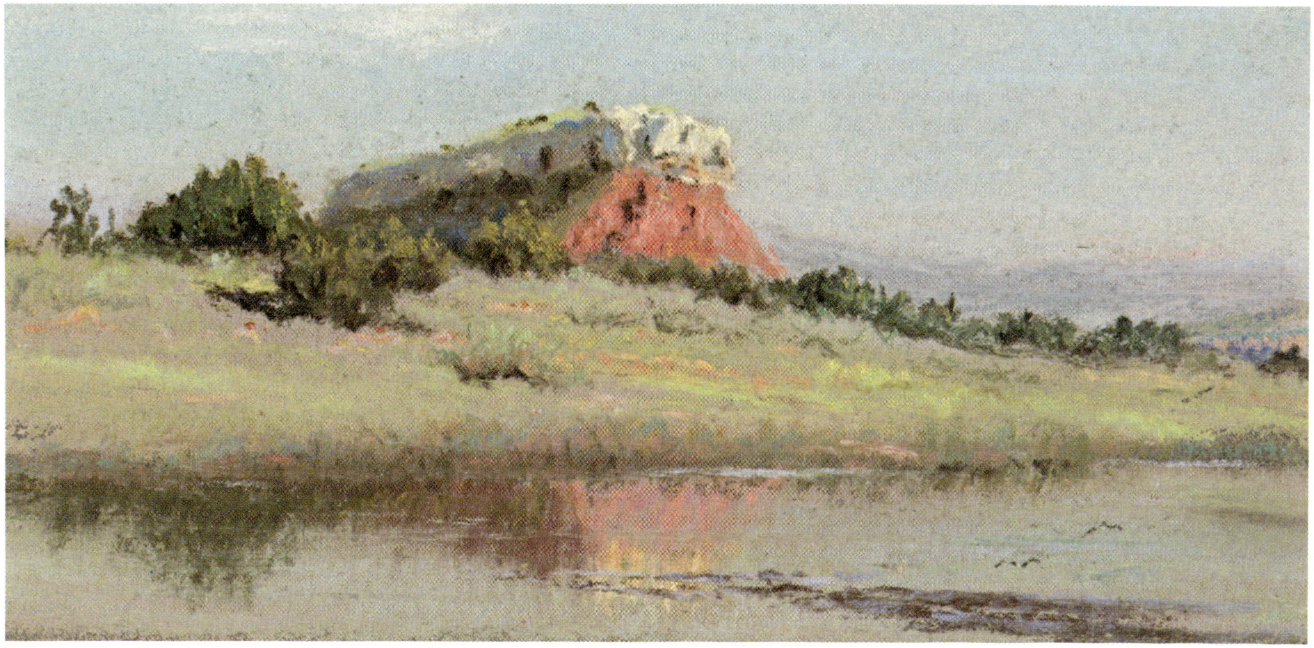

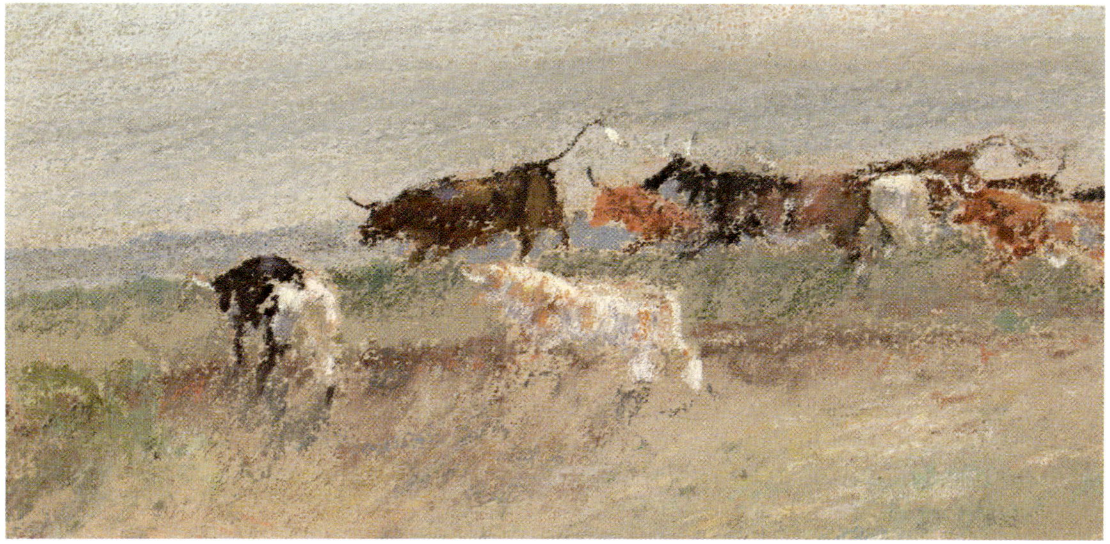

PLATE 56

Afternoon Haze

Pastel

3 ½ × 8

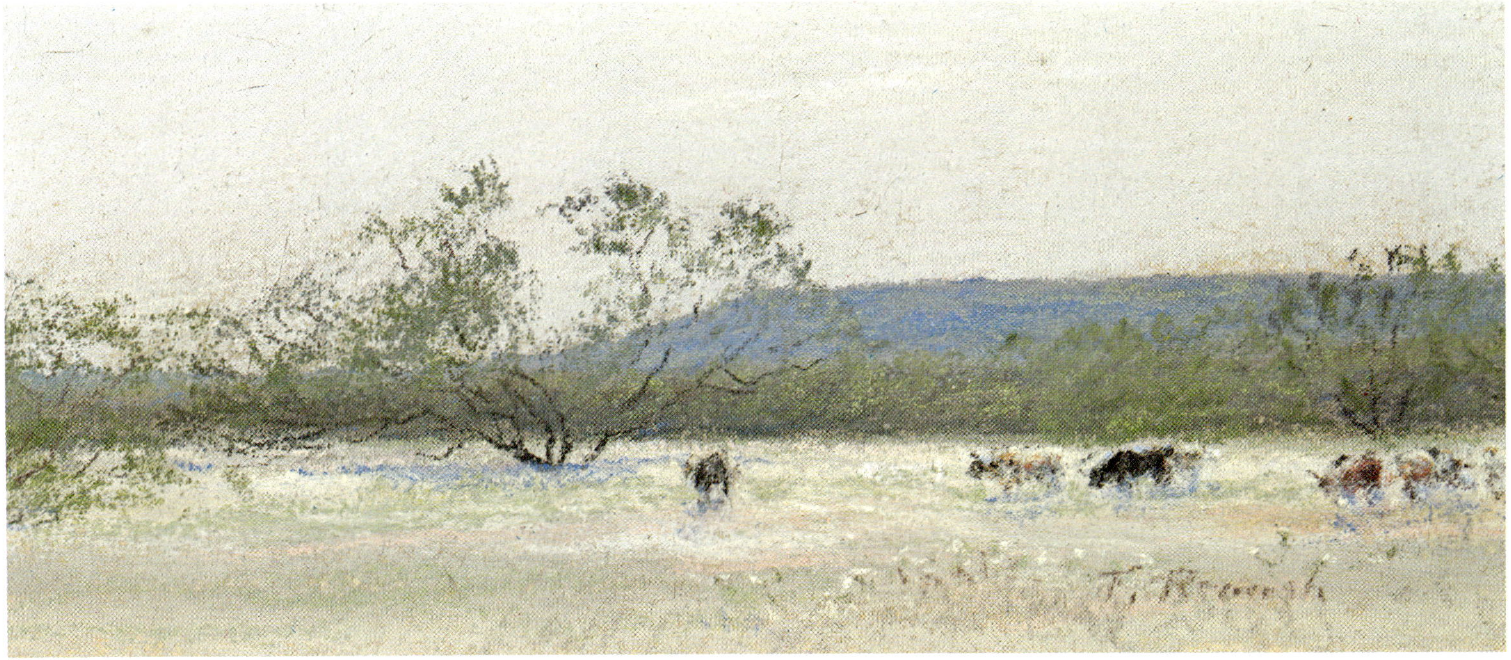

PLATE 57

Weather Prophets

Pastel

3 ½ × 8

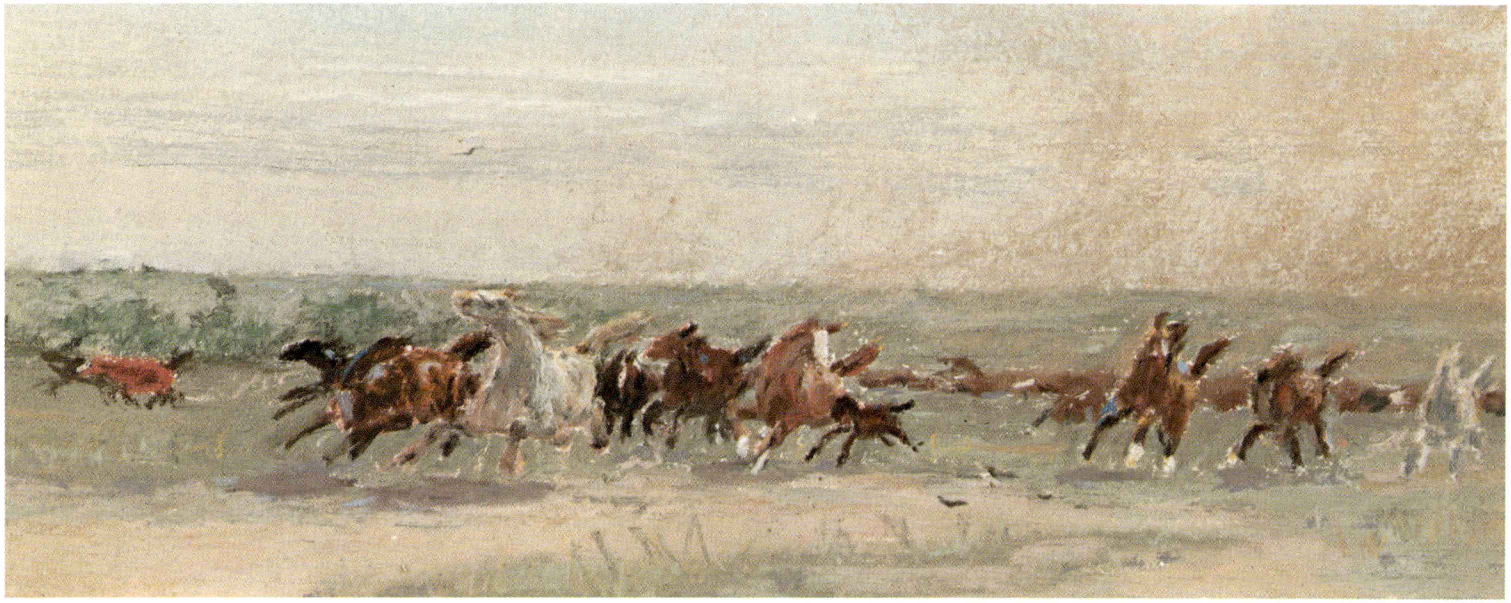

PLATE 58
Mesquite and Pink Butte
Pastel
3 ½ × 6 ½

PLATE 59
Glass Mountains—Big Bend
Pastel
3 ¼ × 7

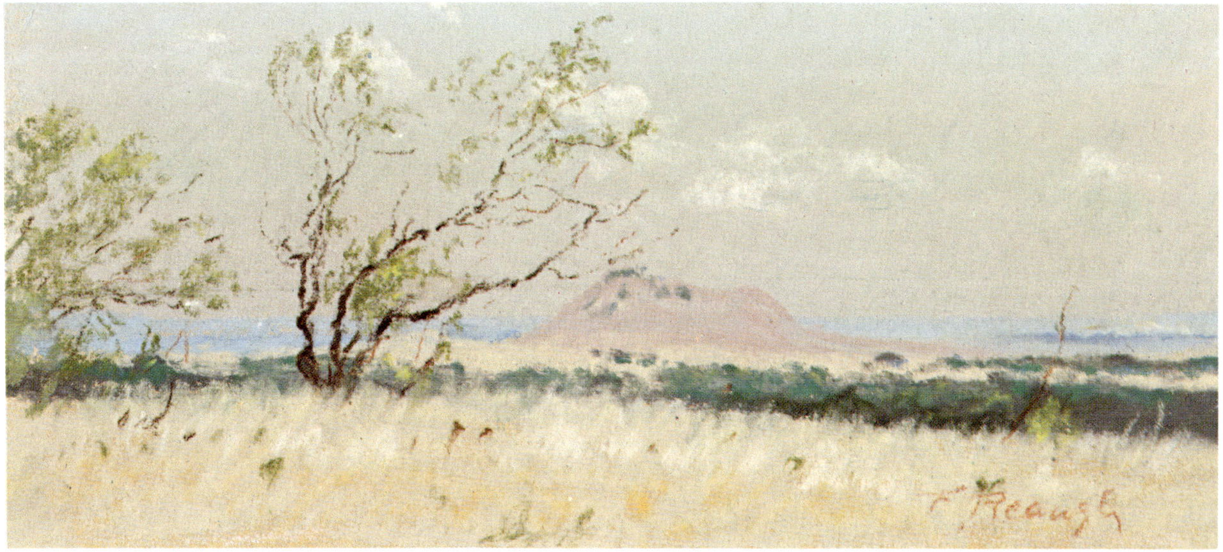
F Reaugh

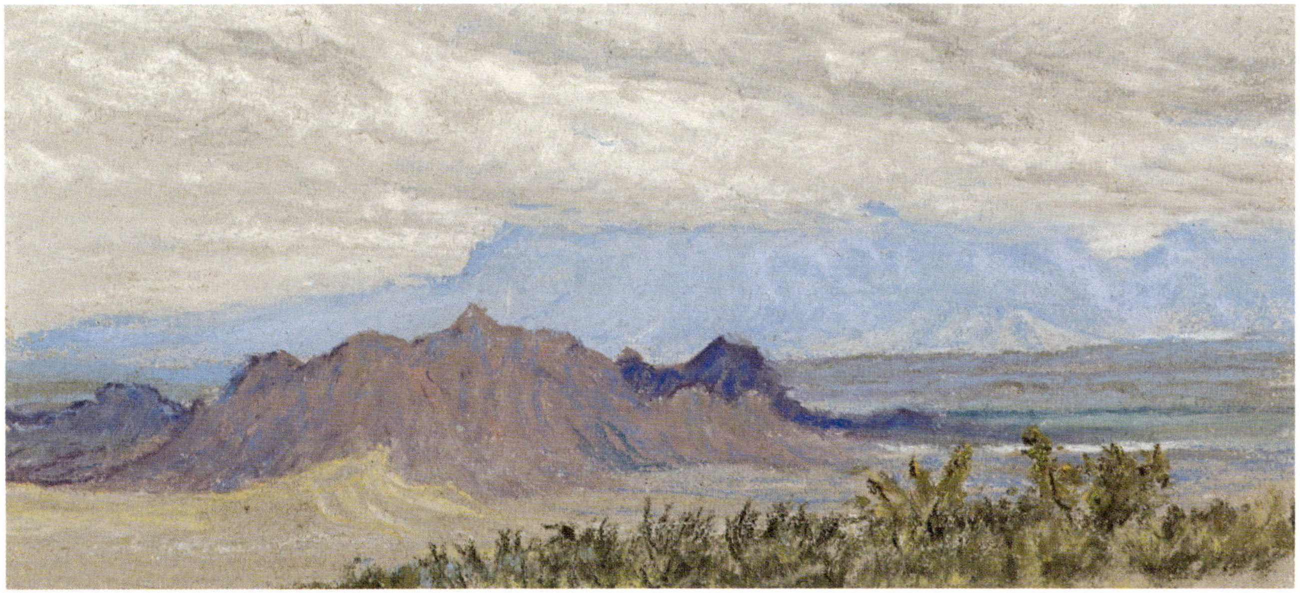

PLATE 60

Cattle in Yucca Country

Pastel

3 ½ × 7 ½

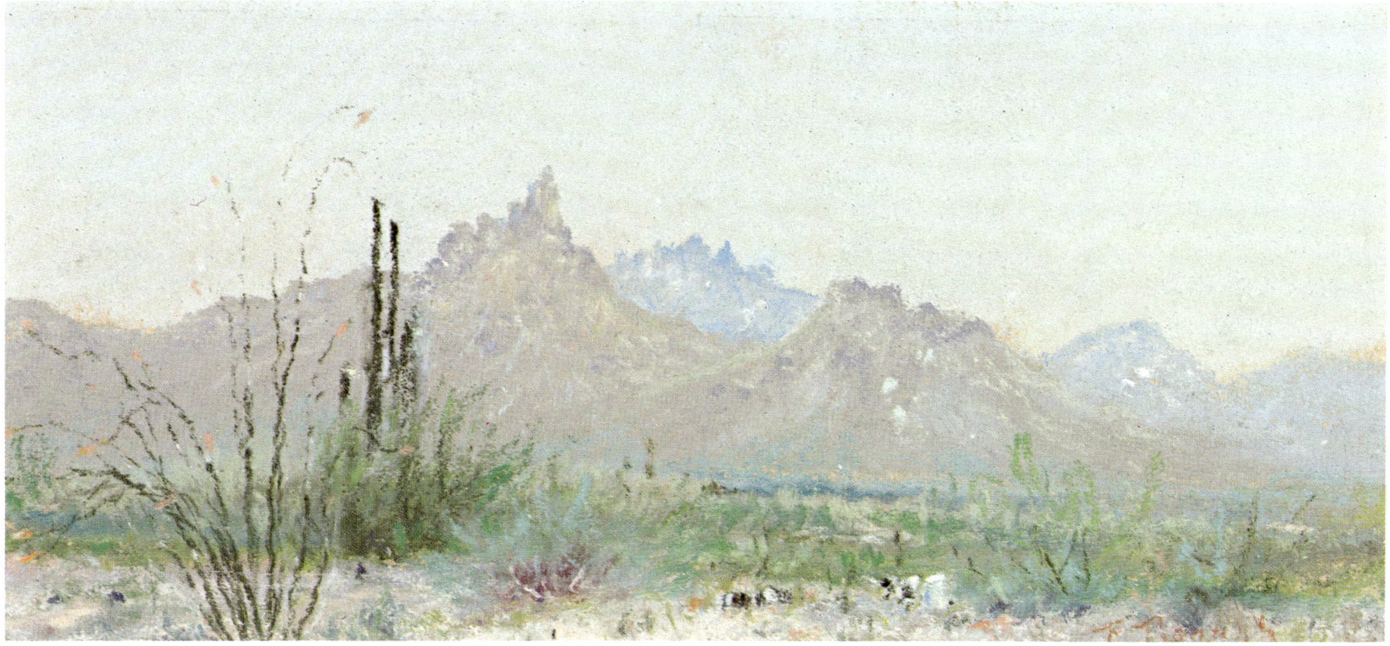

PLATE 61

The Mountain Lion of Tule Canyon

Pastel

3 ¼ × 6 ½

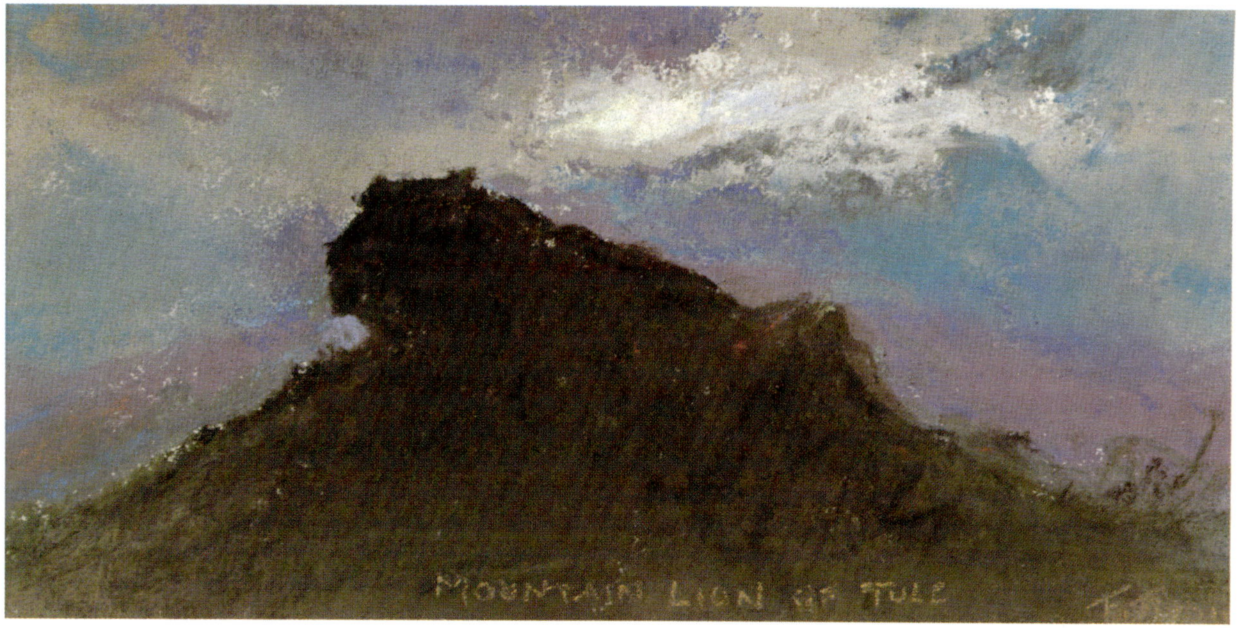
MOUNTAIN LION OF TULE